At the Musician's Table: Food and Music

by
Wendy Horikoshi
Maho Matsui
Fujiko Motoyama

Asahi Press

音声再生アプリ「リスニング・トレーナー」を使った音声ダウンロード

朝日出版社開発のアプリ、「リスニング・トレーナー(リストレ)」を使えば、教科書の音声をスマホ、タブレットに簡単にダウンロードできます。どうぞご活用ください。

◉ アプリ【リスニング・トレーナー】の使い方

《アプリのダウンロード》

App Store または Google Play から「リスニング・トレーナー」のアプリ(無料)をダウンロード

App Storeはこちら▶

Google Playはこちら▶

《アプリの使い方》

① アプリを開き「コンテンツを追加」をタップ
② 画面上部に【15722】を入力しDoneをタップ

音声ストリーミング配信 》》》

この教科書の音声は、右記ウェブサイトにて無料で配信しています。

https://text.asahipress.com/free/english/

Photographs by Aflo(Chapter1～5, 7～14), 大分市歴史資料館 (Chapter6)

は　じ　め　に

　本テキスト *At the Musician's Table: Food and Music*（『音楽家たちが奏でる食文化』）は、*A Taste of English*（『フィクションにみる食文化』）、*A Flavor of English*（『映画で味わう食文化』）、*A View from Painters' Palettes*（『絵画を彩る食文化』）に続く、食文化シリーズの4作目になります。題名が示すとおり、古今東西の著名な音楽家たちの人生と食に纏わるエピソードをテーマとして、読みやすい英語で楽しく学べるように編集されています。

　本テキストに登場する13人の音楽家たちの人生を辿っていると、とても面白いことに気づきました。モーツァルトやショパンに関しては、たくさんの書簡が残されていることは有名ですが、滝廉太郎や小澤征爾氏も、残されている手紙がお二人について知るための貴重な資料の役割を果たしています。一方、現在活躍しているテイラー・スウィフトやビリー・アイリッシュは、SNSなどのソーシャルメディアをうまく活用して、自らの考えを発信し、ファンと気軽に繋がっているのは、まさに時代の変化を反映しています。13人の音楽家たちのジャンルの違いとともに、音楽家たちが生きた時代の変化も楽しんで頂ければ嬉しいです。

　各章は、Reading Passage, Vocabulary Check, Reading Comprehension, Listening Comprehension, Idioms & Expressions, Enjoy the Dialogue! で構成されています。練習問題では、本文の内容の理解を助け、学んだことを活用できる問題作りを目指しました。また、巻末に各章のQuizを用意しています。基礎文法の復習や語彙力の向上に役立てて下さい。

　本書の刊行にあたって、朝日出版社編集部の朝日英一郎氏、小林啓也氏に大変お世話になりました。いつも的確なるご助言を頂いたことに、心より感謝申し上げます。

2024年
著者一同

CONTENTS

At the Musician's Table: Food and Music

Chapter 1 — The Beatles & Strawberry Fields

> ビートルズは1960年代に活躍したイギリス・リバプール出身の4人組ロックグループである。彼らの楽曲は今も世界中で愛されている。

📖 Reading Passage

More than 50 years have passed since the Beatles broke up in 1970. They were, and still are, one of the most popular and influential rock groups to **emerge** in the 1960s. Sadly, two of the four members, John Lennon and George Harrison, are no longer with us. Even today, the Beatles are loved and cited as a major influence on the music world. It is surprising that they were a rock group 5 for only eight short years.

Their debut single, *Love Me Do*, written a few years before, by then teenagers Paul McCartney and John Lennon, was released in 1962. In a short time, they acquired a very large and enthusiastic fan base. The conservatives of the 1960s raised their eyebrows at the Beatles' critical and sometimes contemptuous attitude 10 to authority. The Beatles were considered **rebellious**, but young people, who felt left out and abandoned by a deceptively **affluent** community, embraced their music and their ideas.

The members had always seemed to get on well together, but by the end of 1966, rumors began to circulate that there were **conflicts** and disagreements 15 among them. The rumors were true: in 1970 Paul McCartney announced his departure and John Lennon, George Harrison and Ringo Starr eventually went their own separate ways.

Strawberry Fields Forever, released in 1967, may not be as well-known as *Yesterday* or *Let It Be*, but it is considered to be one of their best songs. Strawberry Field was a Salvation Army orphanage in a suburb of Liverpool. It was near the home of John Lennon's aunt and uncle. He used to live with them as a child. He visited the orphanage's garden, played with his friends in the wooded grounds, and enjoyed garden parties there, every summer. Although the name Strawberry Field **conjures** up images of a happy place, John and the orphans must have felt some sadness and loneliness at not being able to live with their parents.

Strawberries are a popular early summer food in England. At harvest time, people go PYO, or strawberry picking at Pick Your Own farms. In the fields, you can only taste a few, but not eat all the strawberries you pick while there. You have to pay for what you pick and take them home in a punnet, to enjoy them.

'Strawberries and cream' is a traditional British dessert, and about 28 tons of strawberries are **consumed** each year, during the two weeks of the Championships, Wimbledon. The four members of the band, almost all of whom became vegetarians or vegans in their later years, may also have enjoyed 'strawberries and cream'. You might think that the multimedia company **founded** by the Beatles is 'Strawberry', but surprisingly it is 'Apple'.

Do you know how the Beatles got their name? It was coined by combining the word 'beat' with the insect 'beetle'. It's a funny name, just like John, Paul, George and Ringo, who loved music and humor.

📖 **Notes** ━━━━━━━━━━━━━━━━━━━━━━━━━━━━━━━━━━━━━

l. 3 **John Lennon:** ジョン・レノン (1940-1980)、ビートルズのリーダーとして、ボーカル・ギターなどを担当

l. 3 **George Harrison:** ジョージ・ハリスン (1943-2001)、リードギターを担当、ソロに転向後 *My Sweet Lord* などのヒット曲がある

l. 8 **Paul McCartney:** ポール・マッカートニー (1942-)、メインボーカルとベースを担当し、ジョン・レノンと共に数多くの楽曲を作詞作曲した

l. 17 **Ringo Starr:** リンゴ・スター (1940-)、ドラムを担当、リードボーカルを務めることもあった

l. 21 **Salvation Army:** 救世軍 (1865年に設立されたキリスト教の団体、広く慈善活動を行っている)

l. 28 **PYO:** Pick Your Own の略、野菜や果物を自分で収穫して買える農場の掲示のこと

l. 32 **the Championships, Wimbledon:** ウィンブルドン選手権、ロンドンのウィンブルドンで1877年から開催されている世界で最古のテニス大会、日本では全英オープンと呼ばれることもある

☑ Vocabulary Check

Match the following words from the reading passage with their correct definition.

1. emerge ( )   **a.** serious argument about something important

2. rebellious ( )   **b.** start a new business or organization

3. affluent ( )   **c.** come out into view

4. conflict ( )   **d.** eat, drink or use

5. conjure ( )   **e.** not obeying rules or people in authority

6. consume ( )   **f.** make something appear as if by magic

7. found ( )   **g.** prosperous or wealthy

🔍 Reading Comprehension

Circle T if the sentence is true or F if it is false.

[T / F] **1.** The Beatles became very popular soon after the release of their debut single.

[T / F] **2.** Conservative people expressed their displeasure at the Beatles in the 1960s.

[T / F] **3.** Lennon lived in Strawberry Field with his aunt and uncle in his childhood.

[T / F] **4.** You can eat as many strawberries as you like while picking at farms.

[T / F] **5.** Many people enjoy both tennis matches and strawberries and cream at Wimbledon.

🎧 Listening Comprehension

Listen and choose the correct answer.

1. Which area in Liverpool is the orphanage named Strawberry Field located?

(A)   (B)   (C)

2. After you pay for strawberries you pick, how do you take them home?

(A)   (B)   (C)

3. What kind of dessert is strawberries and cream?

(A)   (B)   (C)

Idioms and Expressions

Choose the correct phrase to complete each sentence.

1. He has a really good (   ) the elderly.
2. It's time you recognized that he is (   ) a child.
3. New words are often (   ) influencers and media reports.
4. She doesn't (   ) with her sister.
5. Mother Teresa devoted her life to the poor and sick (   ) society.

> get on well   abandoned by   no longer   coined by   attitude to

Enjoy the Dialogue!

Listen and fill in the blanks in the conversation below.

Olivia: What kind of food do you like?

Luna: Well, I really like my mum's cooking. She makes lots of 1 _____ English desserts.

Olivia: Wow, your mum sounds like a good cook! What's your favorite dessert?

Luna: I love strawberries and cream in the summer. My parents usually take us strawberry picking 2 _____ a year, then we go home, and my mum 3 _____ strawberries and cream and we all watch the tennis 4 _____ .

Olivia: You are so lucky, to have a 5 _____ family. Did I tell you I became a vegetarian last year?

Luna: Really? I didn't know you were a vegetarian. What do you like to make?

Olivia: Well, tonight, I am making vegetarian lasagne. But you have me 6 _____ strawberries and cream. Let's go to the supermarket and get some, and you can come over to my place for dinner.

Luna: Thanks! That sounds great. I will just 7 _____ my coat.

フジコ・ヘミング（1932-　）は数々の苦難を乗り越え、60歳を過ぎてから日本で一大ブームを巻き起こし、その演奏と生き方が多くの人々を魅了するピアニストである。

📖 Reading Passage

11

Fuzjko Hemming is a prominent pianist with a wide and varied career. She is **currently** enjoying popularity around the world, but it wasn't until she was in her 60s that she became well-known in Japan.

12

Hemming was born in Berlin to a Swedish architect father and a Japanese pianist mother in 1932. When she was five years old, her family came back to 5 Japan. Unfortunately, her father returned permanently to Sweden in less than a year. At that time, Japan was not a comfortable place for him to live, because of the **hostile** atmosphere to foreigners. Sadly, she never saw him again.

13

At the age of five Hemming began to take piano lessons from her mother. When she was eighteen, she went through a painful experience. She was 10 **deprived** of her Swedish nationality, because she had never lived there, and she was left stateless. Her dreams of going to Berlin were ruined, but the German ambassador extended her a helping hand. When she got to Berlin, it was as a refugee of the Red Cross, and she entered Germany's national music university in 1961. 15

14

Though Hemming went through **discrimination** and extreme poverty in

Berlin, she would gain the chance to succeed in Vienna in 1970. When her solo concert was planned on Bernstein's recommendation, she was struck down by another **ordeal**. She caught a bad cold and lost her hearing in her left ear. Her bright future turned dark, though she managed to make a living by giving piano lessons in Germany for many years.

In 1996 Hemming began to live in Japan again, where a miracle happened. As soon as her documentary aired on TV, she suddenly attracted the spotlight, and many people were deeply moved by her life story and performances. Presently, every concert is filled with her enthusiastic fans.

Hemming is an ardent animal lover and keeps many cats. She is a vegetarian and especially likes potatoes. In her teenage diary, she wrote about potato pancakes. She cooked simply by mixing grated potatoes and flour, while food was **scarce** just after World War II. Potato pancakes are a common and popular dish in Germany. Every time she cooked potato pancakes, she would have remembered the delicious ones she enjoyed with her father in Berlin, as a little girl.

Hemming experienced the depths of despair and extreme poverty, but has gained fame and wealth. She is now helping many people by lifting their spirits, and contributing to good causes financially. She says she doesn't want perfectionism in her music, but joy, passion and expression above all else. Her life, full of hardships and frustration, has made her performances impressive and touching. By the same token, her love for music, and her care for animals and those less fortunate have made her career much more **captivating**.

🔊 Notes

l. 4 **Berlin:** ベルリン (ドイツ連邦共和国の首都)

l. 4 **a Japanese pianist mother:** 母の大月投網子 (1903-1993) は、東京藝術大学卒業後に音楽留学したベルリンで、フジコの父ジョスタ・ゲオルギー・ヘミングと出会い結婚した

l. 12 **stateless:** 無国籍の

l. 14 **the Red Cross:** 赤十字社 (戦争や災害時における傷病者の救護活動を行う組織、本部はスイス・ジュネーブ)

l. 17 **Vienna:** ウィーン (オーストリアの首都で「音楽の都」とも呼ばれる、モーツァルトやベートーヴェンなど多くの音楽家が活躍した)

l. 18 **Bernstein:** レナード・バーンスタイン (1918-1990)、アメリカの指揮者・作曲家・ピアニスト (クラシックだけでなくミュージカル『ウエスト・サイド物語』の作曲など幅広い分野で活躍した、小澤征爾や佐渡裕も師事した)

l. 29 **World War II:** 第二次世界大戦 (1939-1945)

l. 34 **good causes:** 慈善活動

l. 37 **By the same token:** 同様に

☑ Vocabulary Check

Match the following words from the reading passage with their correct definition.

1. currently ( ) **a.** not easy to find or get
2. hostile ( ) **b.** at the present time
3. deprive ( ) **c.** very attractive and interesting
4. discrimination ( ) **d.** a long, very painful or dreadful experience
5. ordeal ( ) **e.** stop or prevent someone from having or using something
6. scarce ( ) **f.** unfair treatment of specific people and groups
7. captivating ( ) **g.** unfriendly, unpleasant or dangerous

🔍 Reading Comprehension

Circle T if the sentence is true or F if it is false.

[T / F] **1.** When Hemming was five years old, her family came back to Japan without her father.

[T / F] **2.** The German ambassador helped Hemming to go to Germany.

[T / F] **3.** Hemming studied music as an official exchange student in Berlin.

[T / F] **4.** A disease almost fatal to her musical career struck Hemming in Europe.

[T / F] **5.** Hemming likes both fried chicken and potatoes.

🎧 Listening Comprehension

🎧 **Listen and choose the correct answer.**
18

1. When Hemming was deprived of her Swedish nationality, how was she left?
   (A)　　(B)　　(C)

2. How did Hemming make a living in Germany for many years?
   (A)　　(B)　　(C)

3. What does Hemming want in her music?
   (A)　　(B)　　(C)

✎ Idioms and Expressions

Choose the correct phrase to complete each sentence.

1. He will be back in (   ) an hour.
2. Our hero (   ) many perils, sailing across the Pacific in a small boat.
3. The stadium is (   ) enthusiastic sports fans.
4. She greatly (   ) the foundation of the college.
5. My parents want me to be honest (   ).

> contributed to   went through   filled with   less than   above all else

💬 Enjoy the Dialogue!

Listen and fill in the blanks in the conversation below.

🎧 19

Sheena: Hi Mum, we're in Germany. We went for something to eat at a 1 _____ shop. They serve hot meals and beer, not just fresh meat!

Mum: Hello love, good to know you arrived safe and sound. How's Berlin?

Sheena: The city is beautiful, but the meals are humungous. Meats, sauerkraut and a mountain of 2 _____ potatoes, with a dollop of 3 _____ .

Mum: Do they have Kartoffelpuffer? I 4 _____ to eat them as a student there. I still love potato pancakes.

Sheena: No, no potato pancakes today, but so many potatoes. Even the side dish is 5 _____ with an ocean of thick gravy.

Mum: They don't do neat and petite food in Berlin. You'll get used to it.

Sheena: We couldn't help but 6 _____ , when the lady was serving out our main. The plates and the portions are 7 _____ , so heavy and piled high with food.

Mum: It's not the most beautiful, but German food fills you up. Have a good time. Talk to you soon!

Chapter 3 Mozart & the Beef Tongue

『フィガロの結婚』や『魔笛』で知られるヴォルフガング・アマデウス・モーツァルト (1756-1791) は、ウィーン古典派音楽を代表するオーストリアの作曲家である。

📖 Reading Passage

20
No one could deny that Wolfgang Amadeus Mozart is one of history's most prominent and popular classical composers. He was born in Salzburg, Austria in 1756. His father was a violinist and song writer in the Prince-Archbishop of Salzburg's court.

21
At the age of five, Mozart began to compose, and his father believed in his ⁵ son's **prodigious** musical ability. The following year, Mozart set off for his first tour, performing with his father and sister. From then on, he carried on touring and visited many European countries. His father wanted him to be a court musician, and he spent about a third of his life traveling. Unfortunately, his father's wish was not fulfilled. But Mozart's name was **immortalized** in musical history. ¹⁰

22
During his time touring, Mozart met many historical figures. At the age of just six, he gave a performance in the presence of Maria Theresa and Marie Antoinette in Vienna. He was granted an audience with Louis XV in Paris, and with George III in London. Goethe attended his concert, held in Frankfurt in 1763. When Beethoven was sixteen years old, he traveled to visit Mozart's **resi-** ¹⁵ **dence** in Vienna.

Historically, this was a period when a musician's social standing was considered quite low. At invitational performances, musicians were **seldom** seated at the same tables as aristocrats, and certainly never royalty. Mozart often felt he was treated as a servant in the court of Salzburg, even after becoming a well-known performer and composer in Europe. When he was twenty-five years old, he moved to Vienna where he lived for the next ten years, until his death.

In Vienna, Mozart was so popular, he was often invited to **luxurious** dinners by the nobility, as well as the wealthy and affluent. He enjoyed a countless variety of lavish, fancy food, but he still craved the things he ate in his youth. One day, he wrote a letter to his father in Salzburg, asking him to send some beef tongue. He told his father he would present it to an **acquaintance**, in order to reward her for her kindness. When his father sent him salted beef tongue, Mozart used half as a gift, and happily shared the other half for dinner with his wife. He most probably asked his father for beef tongue, for himself.

Mozart made a living by holding concerts, teaching the piano and composing operas in Vienna. He must have earned a fair amount of money. However, partly because of his poor spending habits, he became increasingly financially distressed. Gradually, his popularity began to **decline**, his debts mounted, and his health failed. He died of an illness on December 5th, 1791, at the age of 35.

In the next chapter on Mozart, we touch on the food he tasted and enjoyed in many European cities while traveling.

📑 Notes

l. 2 **Salzburg:** ザルツブルク（ドイツとの国境近くにあるオーストリアの都市）

l. 3 **the Prince-Archbishop of Salzburg:** ザルツブルク大司教

l. 12 **in the presence of …:** 〜の前で

l. 12 **Maria Theresa:** マリア・テレジア（1717-80）、オーストリア大公（在位1740-80）、ハプスブルク家の出身、マリー・アントワネットの母

l. 12 **Marie Antoinette:** マリー・アントワネット（1755-93）、ルイ16世の妃、フランス革命で処刑される

l. 13 **be granted an audience with …:** 〜への謁見(えっけん)を許される

l. 13 **Louis XV:** ルイ15世（1710-74）、ブルボン朝第4代フランス国王（在位1715-74）

l. 14 **George III:** ジョージ3世（1738-1820）、ハノーヴァー朝第3代イギリス国王（在位1760-1820）

l. 14 **Goethe:** ゲーテ（1749-1832）、『若きウェルテルの悩み』（1774）などで知られるドイツの詩人・小説家

l. 14 **Frankfurt:** フランクフルト（ドイツ中西部の商工業都市、ゲーテの生地）

l. 15 **Beethoven:** ルートヴィヒ・ヴァン・ベートーヴェン（1770-1827）、ドイツの作曲家、5章参照

☑ Vocabulary Check

Match the following words from the reading passage with their correct definition.

1. prodigious ( ) **a.** not often or almost never

2. immortalize ( ) **b.** reduce the amount or quality; lessen or weaken

3. residence ( ) **c.** make someore or something famous for a long time

4. seldom ( ) **d.** someone you know, but who is not a close friend

5. luxurious ( ) **e.** extremely impressive, wonderful or amazing

6. acquaintance ( ) **f.** the place where someone lives

7. decline ( ) **g.** very expensive and comfortable

🔍 Reading Comprehension

Circle T if the sentence is true or F if it is false.

[T / F] **1.** After leaving Salzburg, Mozart was eager to taste the food he had eaten there.

[T / F] **2.** Thanks to many concert tours, Mozart was employed as a court musician.

[T / F] **3.** Mozart did not present his acquaintance with the beef tongue his father had sent to him.

[T / F] **4.** As Mozart earned a fair amount of money, he did not experience financial difficulties.

[T / F] **5.** Mozart died in Vienna after he had lived there for ten years.

🎧 Listening Comprehension

Listen and choose the correct answer.

27

1. Why were musicians seldom seated at the same tables as aristocrats at invitational performances?

(A) (B) (C)

2. How did Mozart often feel in the court of Salzburg?

(A) (B) (C)

3. Why did Mozart want to present beef tongue to his acquaintance?

(A) (B) (C)

✎ Idioms and Expressions

Choose the correct phrase to complete each sentence.

1. My mother (   ) for her business trip to Kyoto early this morning.

2. Shall we (   ) with the meeting after the lunch break?

3. He is a fluent speaker of French and Spanish (   ) English.

4. Lots of people were waiting in line (   ) get the newest game system.

5. He closed down his restaurant (   ) a worker shortage.

> in order to   partly because of   as well as   set off   carry on

💬 Enjoy the Dialogue!

Listen and fill in the blanks in the conversation below.

🎧
28

Greg: Do you cook much, Sam?

Sam: Sometimes. I cook maybe ₁ _____ a week, but I'm too busy to do more than that. How about you, Greg?

Greg: I eat out so much, but I want to get into better eating ₂ _____ .

Sam: You're right. Eating out is expensive and unhealthy!

Greg: What do you do the ₃ _____ of the time for lunch and dinner?

Sam: I end up eating ₄ _____ fast food on the way home from work, then I feel bloated.

Greg: I'm the same way, buying ₅ _____ food. Maybe we should both start cooking more?

Sam: Yeah, it's ₆ _____ and will save us some money. We could save the cash for a nice trip away somewhere.

Greg: Let's do a lot of cooking Sunday, at my place, then we'll have food for the week.

Sam: OK! Packed lunches for work, then eat ₇ _____ for dinner? That's a good plan.

演奏旅行でヨーロッパのさまざまな都市を訪れたモーツァルトは、しばしば富裕層や上流階級の食卓に招かれ、当時はまだ珍しかった食べ物でもてなされた。

父レオポルト・姉ナンネルと合奏するモーツァルト

📖 Reading Passage

29

We talked about Mozart in the previous chapter, and how he started his musical career, touring around Europe at the tender age of six. He visited and performed in many European countries: France, Italy, Switzerland, Germany, and England to name a few.

30

During this time, people traveled in horse-drawn carriages. Journeys such as 5 this would have been very hard, sometimes unbearable, for a small child like Mozart, due to rough roads and stone-paved streets. He often **suffered** serious illnesses while traveling from city to city, country to country. It's thought that the rigors of constant touring and performing, during his musical career, are what caused his health to be **fragile** and ultimately cut short his life at 35. 10

31

Mozart's father cared greatly about his son's health, and gave detailed instructions on meals, when the boy would fall ill. But his father was a **thrifty** person and didn't like to spend a lot of money on food. While traveling, Mozart and his father would often make do with simple and inexpensive meals, like dried beef and **stale** rye bread sandwiches. As he became more well-known, he was 15 invited to dine in a much more luxurious manner.

What kinds of things did Mozart like to drink? At that time, the drinking water was not safe. Contamination and general unsanitary conditions meant that even children drank beer or wine, diluted with hot water and so did Mozart. As he grew older, he loved not only beer and wine, but also champagne and punch. He was an avid coffee lover, too.

In a letter to an acquaintance, Mozart's father wrote that his family enjoyed better food in London, than in any other city. They **relished** typical English foods — roast beef and pudding was a staple. Mozart had oysters for the very first time there. In Italy, Mozart encountered various kinds of, at the time, rare and extravagant fruits: pears, peaches and melons. He also enjoyed watermelon with sugar and cinnamon. In the eighteenth century, royalty and nobility had begun to **cultivate** fruits in greenhouses in Europe. Naturally, fruits grown in greenhouses were out of reach for the common people.

Mozart was very fond of sweets. His favorites were lemon peel and raisin pound cake, cheese cake and cookies. He liked strawberry sherbet above anything else, and sherbet and ice cream were very popular desserts at dinner parties held by the upper classes. Mozart was a regular customer at cafés, where he often enjoyed coffee, cakes and lemonade, and his favorite, strawberry sherbet.

Mozart tasted both the simple diet of the common people, and the gorgeous dinners of royalty and nobility. According to his wife, he was not particular about his food. What captivated his heart and occupied his mind most was to **attain** undying fame as a musician. However, if he had known there would be sweets bearing his name, he would have very happily enjoyed them over a cup of coffee at a café.

📖 Notes

l. 5 **horse-drawn carriages:** 馬が引く郵便馬車

l. 7 **stone-paved streets:** 石畳の道

l. 14 **make do with ...:** 〜で間に合わせる

l. 20 **punch:** パンチ（ワインやブランデーなどの洋酒に、果汁・砂糖・レモン・香料などを入れて作る飲み物）

l. 24 **pudding:** プディング（小麦粉・牛乳・卵などを混ぜて作り、ローストビーフに添えて出される）

l. 28 **greenhouse:** 温室

l. 38 **sweets bearing his name:**「モーツァルトトルテ」（チョコレートケーキ）に代表されるように、モーツァルトの死後、彼の人気にあやかって、彼の名前を冠したスイーツがたくさん作られている

☑ Vocabulary Check

Match the following words from the reading passage with their correct definition.

1. suffer   (   )   **a.** succeed in getting something after much effort
2. fragile   (   )   **b.** eat or drink with great pleasure
3. thrifty   (   )   **c.** easily broken or damaged
4. stale   (   )   **d.** prepare and use land for growing plants
5. relish   (   )   **e.** no longer fresh or good to eat
6. cultivate   (   )   **f.** experience pain or illness in body or mind
7. attain   (   )   **g.** using as little money as possible, carefully and wisely

🔍 Reading Comprehension

Circle T if the sentence is true or F if it is false.

[T / F]   **1.** Mozart may have died early, partly because of the long hard journeys he endured at a young age.

[T / F]   **2.** As Mozart's farther cared greatly about his son's health, they always enjoyed luxurious dinners while traveling.

[T / F]   **3.** Mozart had never tasted oysters before he ate them in London.

[T / F]   **4.** In the 18th century farmers cultivated various kinds of fruits on farms in Europe.

[T / F]   **5.** Mozart frequently visited cafés and enjoyed his favorite sweets.

🎧 Listening Comprehension

Listen and choose the correct answer.
36

1. When Mozart fell ill, what did his father do?

    (A)   (B)   (C)

2. When the drinking water was not safe, what did children drink?

    (A)   (B)   (C)

3. How did Mozart enjoy eating watermelon?

    (A)   (B)   (C)

✎ Idioms and Expressions

Choose the correct phrase to complete each sentence. If necessary, change the phrase into the correct grammatical form.

1. The price of lettuce is going up (   ) the poor rainfall this year.

2. He always eats and drinks too much when he goes out, and never seems to (   ) his health.

3. As I don't feel like eating in the morning, I often (   ) a cup of coffee.

4. An around-the-world voyage by luxury cruise liner is (   ) for many people.

5. (   ) the long-term weather forecast, the rainy season will end much later than usual.

> out of reach   according to   make do with   care about   due to

💬 Enjoy the Dialogue!

Listen and fill in the blanks in the conversation below.

🎧 37

Lynne: Let's get some coffee and a sandwich first. I'm 1 _____ !

Marc: Sure, where'd you like to go? There's a swanky boutique place on 5th street, or the café 2 _____ the road.

Lynne: Let's just hit that one. The Wifi is free and I can't stand 3 _____ places. I've been to the one on 5th. It's full of would-be writers and artists, and it's pricey. The area is getting gentrified. This place is family owned.

Marc: OK, it looks pretty 4 _____ . I'll get this one. You paid for my coffee last time.

Lynne: You sure? I'm really hungry. I was planning on getting cake, a sandwich and coffee, just to start! I didn't eat breakfast, and it's almost 2.

Marc: No 5 _____ , Lynne. What do you want?

Lynne: OK, I'll have an extra-large latte with 6 _____ cream, some chocolate cake, a corned beef and salad on rye bread, and a packet of 7 _____ .

Marc: Hahaha wow, you are hungry! I will be right back. How about you get us a table?

「楽聖」と称えられるルートヴィヒ・ヴァン・ベートーヴェン（1770-1827）は、聴覚を失う苦しみと闘いながら、『第九』をはじめとして、数々の名曲を世に送り出した。

📖 Reading Passage

Symphony No. 9, composed by Ludwig van Beethoven in 1824, is one of the world's most recognizable pieces of music. You will hear it played every Christmastime. Much of his work still remains extremely popular, about 200 years after his death. Of all the classical musicians, his works are the most frequently performed.

Beethoven was born in Bonn, Germany in 1770. His grandfather was a conductor and his father a tenor in the royal court. Beethoven was named for his grandfather and believed this was where he **inherited** his great musical talent. His father, an alcoholic with a quick temper, was very strict on him. Early in his young life, an organist at the court took Beethoven under his wing, and helped him to **improve** his musical ability.

In 1786 Beethoven made his first visit to Vienna, to see Mozart at his residence. The visit was cut short, and he was obliged to go back to Bonn, following news of his mother's illness. He stayed in Vienna only two weeks. Returning home, he worked very hard, supporting his family while his father was unable. Six years later he visited Vienna again, and decided to settle there permanently.

Beethoven became known as a virtuoso pianist in Vienna, and soon was **established** as a prominent composer. As his fame was beginning to spread, his worries over his hearing became a great concern in his late-20s. He despaired in the **agony** of losing his hearing. Though he suffered from difficulties with his ₂₀ hearing until his death, he overcame his struggles, including thoughts of suicide, and went on to have his career peak in his mid-30s.

It appears that Beethoven was not a gourmet, but he was very particular about coffee and eggs. Coffee was his favorite beverage second only to wine. It was his habit to roast coffee beans, grinding them with a mill, to make coffee for ₂₅ himself every morning. The exact number of beans was always 60. He was remarkably particular about the freshness of eggs. When his maid brought him a rotten egg, he threw it back at her in a fit of rage and disgust. He sometimes cooked for himself, and occasionally for his guests. It is said that his friends were very perplexed by his poor culinary skills when they were invited to dinner. ₃₀

Although Beethoven remained single, three love letters were found unmailed in his desk after his death. He gave piano lessons to aristocratic women, and may have fallen in love with a few of them. He had a difficult and **stubborn** personality as an artist. It's sad to think that he never married one of his great loves, due to this, and differences in social class at the time. On his death at the age of 56, ₃₅ he was greatly **mourned**. Vienna had lost a master composer!

According to a ballot by a famous music magazine, Beethoven was elected as the most popular classical composer in Japan. 2020 was the 250th anniversary of his birth, **muted** by the pandemic. Let's hope for a huge celebration on his 300th! ₄₀

📖 **Notes** ━━━━━━━━━━━━━━━

l. 1 **Symphony No. 9:** 交響曲第9番ニ短調作品125、ベートーヴェンが1824年に作曲した独唱と合唱を伴う交響曲、日本では略して『第九』と呼ばれる

l. 6 **Bonn:** ボン（ドイツ中西部の都市、1949年から1990年まで西ドイツの首都だった）

l. 24 **second only to …:** 〜を除いて

l. 37 **ballot:** 無記名投票

☑ Vocabulary Check

Match the following words from the reading passage with their correct definition.

1. inherit ( ) **a.** perform well, and have it recognized and accepted
2. improve ( ) **b.** extreme mental or physical pain
3. establish ( ) **c.** tone down or subdue
4. agony ( ) **d.** feel or show deep sadness
5. stubborn ( ) **e.** receive something from someone who has died
6. mourn ( ) **f.** unwilling to change one's mind
7. mute ( ) **g.** make something better

🔍 Reading Comprehension

Circle T if the sentence is true or F if it is false.

[T / F] **1.** Beethoven believed he inherited his great musical talent from his father.

[T / F] **2.** Beethoven could not see Mozart at his first visit to Vienna.

[T / F] **3.** Overcoming the fear of losing his hearing, Beethoven reached the peak of his career in his 30s.

[T / F] **4.** Beethoven sometimes cooked for himself, but was not a good cook.

[T / F] **5.** Beethoven gave piano lessons to aristocratic women, and got married to one of them.

🎧 Listening Comprehension

Listen and choose the correct answer.

45

1. When Beethoven made his first visit to Vienna, why was he obliged to go back to Bonn soon?

(A)   (B)   (C)

2. When his maid brought him a rotten egg, what did Beethoven do?

(A)   (B)   (C)

3. When Beethoven invited his friends to dinner, what did they think of his cooking?

(A)   (B)   (C)

✍ Idioms and Expressions

Choose the correct phrase to complete each sentence.

1. Owing to the pandemic, my sister was (   ) give up going to Italy for her fine arts degree.

2. Coffee is her favorite beverage, and she is very (   ) how it's made.

3. We often make mistakes when we decide things (   ) anger.

4. We were very (   ) the sudden, unexpected cancellation of the music festival.

5. She was (   ) the next President of our university.

> perplexed by   in a fit of   particular about   elected as   obliged to

💬 Enjoy the Dialogue!

Listen and fill in the blanks in the conversation below.

🎧
46

Mario: Hi Andy, what are you bringing to the Potluck party tonight?

Andy: Hi Mario, I thought I would make some Tiramisu. It's my favorite Italian dessert.

Mario: That sounds 1 _____ . I love Italian food. I am making a 2 _____ Timballo.

Andy: What's in Timballo? I have never 3 _____ of it.

Mario: Pasta, eggs, about four kinds of cheese, aubergine, tomato, 4 _____ meat and spices, and some other 5 _____ . It's my grandmother's secret family 6 _____ . She's a great cook.

Andy: You are so lucky to have an Italian grandma! Do you know what anyone else is bringing?

Mario: Yeah, Annie is doing a vinaigrette salad, George is cooking Grissini from 7 _____ , and Salma is making Arancini.

Andy: Looks like I am the only one bringing a dessert then. I hope we do Italian Potluck night again. It's so good for finding out about new food.

Chapter 6　Rentaro Taki & Fukujinzuke

『荒城の月』『箱根八里』『花』などで知られる滝廉太郎（1879-1903）は、明治時代の日本の西洋音楽草創期に活躍し、将来を嘱望されながら早世した作曲家である。

帰国する滝廉太郎（前列左から2人目）のためにライプツィヒ在住の日本人留学生たちが催した送別会にて

📖 Reading Passage

47
　　In the winter of 1901, Rentaro Taki caught a severe cold, and was admitted to hospital in Leipzig, Germany. It had been about two months since he entered the Leipzig Conservatory. He had been sent as an official student to Europe, by the Japanese government. As only the third person to study music abroad in the Meiji period, this was a great honor. 5

48
　　During his eight months in hospital, his health **deteriorated** further, and in the following year, with little improvement in his condition, he was forced to re-turn home to Japan. He had only been studying in Germany a year and three months, and his ill health cut short his **ambitions** in Europe. Eight months after his return to Japan, he sadly died of tuberculosis at the age of 23. With no cure 10 for the disease at that time, many young people were dying from it. His sudden death was a **huge** loss for music education in the Meiji period.

49
　　Born in Tokyo in 1879, Rentaro spent his childhood in Yokohama, Toyama and Oita, where his father worked as a clerk. After eight years of schooling, he moved to Tokyo from Taketa to study music. Six months later, as the youngest 15 student ever to **qualify**, he entered the Tokyo Music School at the age of 15.

Rentaro made every effort to keep up with the lessons. With rapidly improving skills, he became highly respected as a brilliant performer on the piano with a beautiful tenor voice. His warmth and mischievousness **endeared** him to everyone. As a research student, he was so quick and talented that he was put in charge 20 of giving piano lessons to other students. Blessed with good teachers and good friends, he had a very happy student life.

At this point in history, music education was not well established in Japan. There was a growing desire to have pupils sing songs by Japanese composers. Rentaro entered the contest, and *Kojo no Tsuki* and *Hakone-Hachiri* were adopted as 25 songs for junior high school music classes. *Hana* was also composed around the same time. Many of you would have sung or heard them in your music classes. He composed them in a very short time, before he left for Germany.

When Rentaro was in Leipzig, about 15 other Japanese students were studying medicine and literature there. As his friends, they were very concerned for his 30 health and took good care of him. One day, Rentaro asked for *fukujinzuke* pickles, and a Japanese student who was studying in Berlin, **delivered** them to his bedside. Did the pickles he received cheer him up? Or did they make him homesick, missing his family and Japan even more? His friends hoped he would recover and return to study with them again in Leipzig, but their wish was not to be **fulfilled**. 35

To commemorate the centenary of Rentaro's death and his contribution to music, a monument was erected on the streets of Leipzig in 2003. Although he had a short career and died too young, his great works will never be forgotten.

📖 Notes

l. 3 **Leipzig Conservatory:** ライプツィヒ音楽院

l. 14 **his father:** 滝家は江戸時代には代々日出藩（大分県）の家老職にあった家柄である、廉太郎の父吉弘は明治政府で大久保利通の秘書を務めた

l. 15 **Taketa:** 現在の大分県竹田市、『荒城の月』は竹田市にある岡城址をイメージしながら作曲したと言われている

l. 16 **Tokyo Music School:** 東京音楽学校（東京藝術大学音楽学部の前身）

l. 28 **Kojo no Tsuki:** 『荒城の月』(1901) 土井晩翠作詞、滝廉太郎作曲

l. 28 **Hakone-Hachiri:** 『箱根八里』(1901) 鳥居忱作詞、滝廉太郎作詞

l. 29 **Hana:** 『花』(1900) 武島羽衣作詞、滝廉太郎作曲

☑ Vocabulary Check

Match the following words from the reading passage with their correct definition.

1. deteriorate ( )   **a.** make someone like you or love you
2. ambition ( )   **b.** do or achieve what is expected
3. huge ( )   **c.** take something to a person or place
4. qualify ( )   **d.** get worse
5. endear ( )   **e.** a strong desire to be successful
6. deliver ( )   **f.** become officially recognized at a profession or activity
7. fulfill ( )   **g.** extremely large

🔍 Reading Comprehension

Circle T if the sentence is true or F if it is false.

[T / F]   **1.** Rentaro was the first to study music abroad in the Meiji period.

[T / F]   **2.** It was easy for Rentaro to keep up with the classes at the Tokyo Music School.

[T / F]   **3.** Rentaro was not only an excellent pianist but also an excellent singer.

[T / F]   **4.** Before Rentaro composed *Kojo no Tsuki*, there were very few songs by Japanese composers.

[T / F]   **5.** In Leipzig Rentaro received *Fukujinzuke* his family sent him from Japan.

🎧 Listening Comprehension

🎧 **Listen and choose the correct answer.**
54

1. Why was Rentaro forced to return home to Japan?
    (A)   (B)   (C)

2. What endeared Rentaro to everyone?
    (A)   (B)   (C)

3. In the Meiji period, what kinds of songs did people want pupils to sing at school?
    (A)   (B)   (C)

✍ Idioms and Expressions

Choose the correct phrase to complete each sentence.

1. She was (   ) the most prestigious ballet company in Europe.

2. Many doctors are seeking a (   ) Alzheimer's disease.

3. She will be (   ) this new project.

4. This practice has been (   ) standard service by many big banks.

5. We are very (   ) the safety of children who walk to school.

> in charge of   admitted to   cure for   concerned for   adopted as

💬 Enjoy the Dialogue!

Listen and fill in the blanks in the conversation below.

🎧 55

Yuki: This is a long drive. Let's pick some music to listen to, while we're in the car.

Dan: Sure! How about Hip Hop? I have a 1 ＿＿＿＿＿＿＿＿＿ of songs on my phone.

Yuki: Nah, I can never understand what they're saying. How about some Metal or Dance music? I have a good club mix on my 2 ＿＿＿＿＿＿＿＿＿ , and the car has Bluetooth.

Dan: I love Metal, but the last two times I got a ticket for 3 ＿＿＿＿＿＿＿＿＿ . I had Megadeth blasting, so that's a hard no.

Yuki: Alright, here's the plan: I pick the tunes, and we put it on 4 ＿＿＿＿＿＿＿＿＿ , and you can pick the snacks, OK?

Dan: It's a 5 ＿＿＿＿＿＿＿＿＿ . I'll grab some at the store just around the corner. Do you want anything in 6 ＿＿＿＿＿＿＿＿＿ ?

Yuki: Yeah, can you get me some pickle chips? The big bag, and a diet Coke.

Dan: You eat pickle chips? That's a really weird 7 ＿＿＿＿＿＿＿＿＿ , but OK.

ミニ情報：幸田姉妹と廉太郎

滝廉太郎は、幸田延（1870-1946）、幸田幸（1878-1963）姉妹に続き、音楽家として3人目の留学生であった。幸田姉妹は明治の文豪幸田露伴（1867-1947）の妹である。

入院中の廉太郎に福神漬けを送ったのは、当時ベルリンに留学していた幸田幸である。

Chapter 7　Frédéric Chopin & Pot-au-feu

「ピアノの詩人」と呼ばれるフレデリック・ショパン（1810-1849）は、故国ポーランドへの強い望郷の思いを募らせながら、パリで活躍した音楽家である。

ドラクロワが描いた
ショパンの肖像画

📖 Reading Passage

56

Have you ever heard of the International Chopin Piano Competition, which is held every five years in Warsaw, Poland? Started in 1927, it's the oldest piano competition in the world. Contestants are required to **exclusively** play pieces by Frédéric Chopin.

57

Born in 1810 in a small village near Warsaw, Chopin was the son of a French 5 father and a Polish mother. His father was a French teacher and played the violin and flute with great skill. His mother, an impressive singer and pianist, was the one who first taught her son to play. Chopin's father recognized his son's extraordinary musical talent at an early age, but wanted him to **acquire** a wide range of knowledge and to become cultured. 10

58

After graduating from the Warsaw Conservatory in 1829, Chopin traveled with his friends to Vienna. There he gave a piano concert to great success. The following year, at the age of 20, he left Warsaw to live in Vienna. However, contrary to his expectations, he did not receive a warm welcome there at all, as the uprising in Poland, happening shortly after Chopin's departure from Warsaw, 15 created bad feelings towards the Poles. Having given up on his dreams for success in Vienna, Chopin left for Paris in 1831.

Paris was home to many **exiled** Poles. Before long, he was invited to the salons of the wealthy and aristocratic, where he gave elegant piano performances. He became one of the most sought-after piano teachers in Paris, achieving finan- 20 cial security. He cultivated friendships with Mendelssohn, Heine, Delacroix and Liszt. One day, Liszt introduced him to a woman named George Sand, a famous feminist. At first, her cigar smoking, manly behavior and clothes made a poor impression on Chopin. They gradually became attracted to each other, and even- tually began to live together in 1838. 25

Sand was **devoted** to Chopin, who was in poor health. He had been suffer- ing from tuberculosis for years. He was a light eater, and didn't have a strong stomach, so Sand took great care of his diet. He **preferred** fish to meat and enjoyed light fish dishes with a glass of wine. Perhaps, Sand would have cooked a pot-au-feu for him by boiling fish and vegetables. Due to her devotion, he 30 survived ill health and was able to concentrate on his musical career.

Sadly, the relationship between Chopin and Sand came to an end in 1847, when he fell into a state of intense **anxiety** and deep loneliness. The following year, escaping the chaos of the February Revolution, he went on a concert tour of England, where he played before Queen Victoria. When he returned to Paris, he 35 was completely **exhausted**. His dramatic life ended, following a series of illness- es, in 1849 at the age of 39.

After his funeral, his sister took his heart back to Warsaw in accordance with his will, and Chopin, who had left Poland at the age of 20, finally returned to his beloved native land, after 20 years away. 40

📖 Notes

l. 1 **International Chopin Piano Competition:** フレデリック・ショパン国際ピアノコンクール（ポーランドのワルシャワで5年ごとに開催される国際音楽コンクール）

l. 11 **Warsaw Conservatory:** ワルシャワ音楽院

l. 20 **sought-after:** 人気のある

l. 22 **Liszt:** フランツ・リスト (1811-1886)、ハンガリー王国出身の作曲家・ピアニスト、超絶的な演奏で「ピアノの魔術師」と呼ばれた

l. 22 **George Sand:** ジョルジュ・サンド (1804-1876)、フランスの作家

l. 35 **Queen Victoria:** ヴィクトリア女王 (1819-1901)、イギリス女王 (在位1837-1901)

l. 38 **his heart:** ショパンの心臓、ワルシャワ市内の教会に安置されている

l. 38 **in accordance with his will:** ショパンの遺言のとおりに

☑ Vocabulary Check

Match the following words from the reading passage with their correct definition.

1. exclusively ( )   **a.** uneasiness, nervousness or fear
2. acquire ( )   **b.** like better or best
3. exiled ( )   **c.** limited to one or only a few things or people
4. devote ( )   **d.** forced to live away from your home country
5. prefer ( )   **e.** extremely tired or completely used up
6. anxiety ( )   **f.** get or attain something
7. exhausted ( )   **g.** give all your time and energy for one purpose

🔍 Reading Comprehension

Circle T if the sentence is true or F if it is false.

[T / F]   **1.** Chopin's parents were both music lovers, and his mother was his first piano teacher.

[T / F]   **2.** Chopin was very disappointed in the people of Vienna, when he visited there again at the age of 20.

[T / F]   **3.** Chopin achieved financial security with piano concerts in big halls in Paris.

[T / F]   **4.** Chopin fell in love with George Sand at first sight.

[T / F]   **5.** Thanks to Sand's devotion to him, Chopin survived ill health.

🎧 Listening Comprehension

Listen and choose the correct answer.

63

1. What were the nationalities of Chopin's parents?

   (A)   (B)   (C)

2. Why did Chopin leave Vienna for Paris in 1831?

   (A)   (B)   (C)

3. Why at first did Chopin have such a poor impression of George Sand?

   (A)   (B)   (C)

✍ Idioms and Expressions

Choose the correct phrase to complete each sentence. If necessary, change the phrase into the correct grammatical form.

1. If you want to visit this art exhibition, you are (   ) reserve a ticket.

2. (   ) popular belief, carrots do not make your eyesight better. It's a myth.

3. (   ) it'll be rainy season. You better buy yourself a nice umbrella.

4. With the exams just around the corner, I have to (   ) studying.

5. The game went into extra innings, but when it (   ) it was still a draw.

> concentrate on   came to an end   required to   before long   contrary to

💬 Enjoy the Dialogue!

Listen and fill in the blanks in the conversation below.

🎧 64

Lucy: Hey Jayden! I didn't see you in class this morning. Were you 1 _____ or did you skip class?

Jayden: Oh, hi Lucy, I wasn't skipping. I was at dress 2 _____ for our orchestra's 3 _____ tomorrow night. As a 4 _____ of fact, I'd really like you to come.

Lucy: Sure. I'd love to. What are you playing this time?

Jayden: We're performing Chopin, opus number 9. I'm playing the Nocturn in B flat minor. It's one of the most 5 _____ piano pieces.

Lucy: I love Chopin! I'll be there in the front 6 _____ . Want to get some coffee with me after? Or maybe some dinner?

Jayden: Well, yeah sure. Um, are you asking me on a date?

Lucy: Yes, I am. It'll be fun! So, coffee or dinner? Or, is that a no?

Jayden: Oh, that's a 7 _____ yes!

ミニ情報：ショパンと交流のあった芸術家

Mendelssohn: フェリックス・メンデルスゾーン（1809-1847）、ドイツのロマン派の作曲家

Heine: ハインリヒ・ハイネ（1797-1856）、ドイツの詩人（歌曲『ローレライ』の作詞者）

Delacroix: ウジェーヌ・ドラクロワ（1798-1863）、フランスのロマン主義を代表する画家、《民衆を導く自由の女神》《キオス島の虐殺》などで知られる

Chapter 8 Antonin Dvořák & his Last Dinner

『スラブ舞曲』や『新世界より』などで知られるアントニン・ドヴォルザーク（1841-1904）は、スメタナ（1824-84）とともにボヘミアを代表する作曲家である。

📖 Reading Passage

Disc 2
1

The first performance of Antonin Dvořák's *From the New World* took place in Carnegie Hall in New York in 1893. The American audience was deeply impressed, and the concert was a huge success. The **previous** year, Dvořák had been invited to the USA to teach at the National Conservatory of Music as its director. He was treated very well, and introduced to Black American and also 5 Native American music while he was there. However, Dvořák missed his country greatly, suffering from homesickness. After staying in America for a little less than three years, he returned home with his family.

2

Dvořák was born in 1841 in a small village in Bohemia, near Prague. His father was a butcher and innkeeper, and was well known as a skilled amateur 10 violin player. As a child, Dvořák sang in the **choir** and played the violin with his father at village celebrations. His father wanted him to have a practical profession, and also to enjoy music as much as he did. Dvořák was a **dutiful** son, so he obediently trained to become a butcher and learned German. Fortunately for him, his German teacher, who was himself quite an accomplished musician, 15 **persuaded** his father to send him to music school instead.

After graduating from a Prague organ school in 1859, Dvořák joined a small orchestra as a viola player. A couple of years later, he joined the orchestra attached to the National Theatre. Shortly after this, Bedřich Smetana was **appointed** conductor of the theater, and Dvořák was strongly influenced by his musical style. 20

 Despite his hard work as a musician, Dvořák was unable to **escape** from financial difficulties. But he was fortunate enough to be awarded a public scholarship in 1875. Brahms was a member of the selection committee, and he spoke highly of Dvořák's musical talent. They **admired** each other and their relationship, like that of a father and son, continued throughout their lives. 25

 On his return from America in 1895, Dvořák began teaching again at the Prague Conservatory, and he received many honors. He traveled to foreign countries, and gave successful concerts, but he preferred to spend time at home with his family, rather than attend parties. Sometimes he worked at the kitchen table, 30 and sometimes he would take a walk to the nearby train station, to relax and enjoy watching the trains.

The Czechs love their beer, and Dvořák was of course a great beer lover. He would have loved Czech home cooking as well. One of the most famous Czech dishes, is roast pork, pickled cabbage and knedlíky. Knedlíky are dumplings that 35 are kneaded, then steamed or boiled. The dough is then sliced like bread.

On 1 May 1904, Dvořák, who had been quite ill, suddenly felt much better. He went to the table to dine with his wife and children, only eating a bowl of soup, but it was to be his final dinner. How fitting that he got to have his last meal, peacefully at home with his beloved family! He was laid to rest in the Prague 40 cemetery, where Smetana also lies.

📖 Notes

l. 2 **Carnegie Hall:** カーネギー・ホール（ニューヨーク市マンハッタンにあるコンサートホール）

l. 4 **National Conservatory of Music:** ニューヨーク・ナショナル音楽院（1885-1952）

l. 9 **Bohemia:** ボヘミア（チェコ西部の地方）

l. 9 **Prague:** プラハ（チェコ共和国の首都）

l. 14 **learned German:** 肉屋の職人としての資格を取得するには、ドイツ語の習得が必須であった

l. 28 **Prague Conservatory:** プラハ音楽院

l. 32 **watching the trains:** 幼少期から鉄道好きだったドヴォルザークは、駅に行って列車を眺めて過ごすのが楽しみであった

l. 35 **knedlíky:** クネドリーキ（茹でて作るチェコの伝統的なパン）

☑ Vocabulary Check

Match the following words from the reading passage with their correct definition.

1. previous ( )   **a.** make someone agree to do something
2. choir ( )   **b.** get away from something
3. dutiful ( )   **c.** choose someone for a job or position
4. persuade ( )   **d.** happening before
5. appoint ( )   **e.** a group of singers in a church or public performance
6. escape ( )   **f.** like and respect greatly
7. admire ( )   **g.** obedient and conscientious

🔍 Reading Comprehension

Circle T if the sentence is true or F if it is false.

[T / F]   **1.** Dvořák applied for a position as the director of an American music school.

[T / F]   **2.** Dvořák was unwilling to train to become a butcher.

[T / F]   **3.** Smetana and Dvořák belonged to the same orchestra for some time.

[T / F]   **4.** Brahms thought Dvořák was suitable for a scholarship.

[T / F]   **5.** After his return from America, Dvořák was warmly welcomed and treated with respect by his home country.

🎧 Listening Comprehension

Listen and choose the correct answer.

8

1. Why did Dvořák return home after staying in America for a little less than three years?

     (A)   (B)   (C)

2. What did his father want Dvořák to do in the future?

     (A)   (B)   (C)

3. What did Dvořák do to relax?

     (A)   (B)   (C)

✍ Idioms and Expressions

Choose the correct phrase to complete each sentence.

1. His concert, which (   ) after a three-year absence, was a big success.

2. The research laboratory is (   ) a famous pharmaceutical company.

3. This hall is large (   ) accommodate up to three thousand people.

4. Many newspapers (   ) her piano performance last month.

5. Her handwriting is very similar to (   ) her mother.

> that of   took place   spoke highly of   attached to   enough to

💬 Enjoy the Dialogue!

Listen and fill in the blanks in the conversation below.

🎧 9

Tomas: Last week I got to travel back to my home town. It was weird being back there after so many years.

Marek: What was weird about it? I always thought you were a very traditional 1 ———————————— .

Tomas: Hmm well, I got a lot of comments about my 2 ———————————— , and when I had dinner with the whole family, about how much beer I drank.

Marek: You've lived here in the States too long. How much beer did you drink?

Tomas: 3 ———————————— to my grandfather, not enough! I had two with dinner, and 4 ———————————— a soda.

Marek: Was that the only strange thing?

Tomas: No. My family 5 ———————————— about how I'm not married. My grandmother says I'm too 6 ———————————— .

Marek: So, you aren't a 7 ———————————— grandson? So what!

ミニ情報：ドヴォルザークに影響を与えた音楽家

Bedřich Smetana: ベドルジハ・スメタナ（1824-1884）、チェコ国民楽派の創始者であるボヘミア生まれの作曲家、代表作に『わが祖国』『売られた花嫁』など

Brahms: ヨハネス・ブラームス（1833-1897）、ドイツの作曲家（バッハ・ベートーヴェンと共にドイツ音楽の「三大B」と称される）

Chapter 9　Elvis Presley & the Elvis Sandwich

「キング・オブ・ロックンロール」と称されたエルビス・プレスリー（1935-1977）
は、戦後アメリカの最大のソロ・アーティストで、世界的な人気を博した。

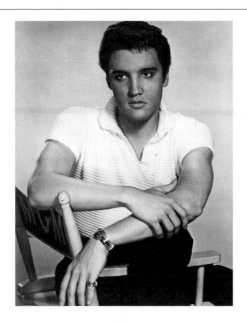

📖 Reading Passage

10

Elvis Presley became the embodiment of the American dream, and was
known as the "King of Rock 'n' Roll". The Beatles, Bob Dylan, Freddie Mercury
and many other musicians were inspired by his music and strongly influenced by
his style. He **achieved** the greatest goals of his life: escaping poverty and making
his beloved mother happy. However, his success story often seems to be **tinged**　5
with sorrow.

11

Presley was born in Tupelo, Mississippi, in 1935, to a young couple. His family was very poor, but he was loved by his parents, especially his mother. At the
age of 13, his family moved to Memphis, Tennessee, which was very fortunate for
him. There he was exposed to a variety of music, including country music,　10
rhythm and blues and gospel.

12

After graduating from high school in 1953, Presley worked as a truck driver.
One day he made a record at his own expense for a small local record company.
Two years later he was signed by a major record label and released his first single,
Heartbreak Hotel. Radio stations were inundated with requests for his songs, his　15
television appearances were highly rated and concert halls were filled with

enthusiastic, screaming female fans. Conservative people **disapproved** of his flamboyant performances on stage and the enthusiasm of his fans. He quickly rose to star status, despite this.

In 1958, at the height of his popularity, Presley enlisted in the army. After   20
two years of military service, he returned to the stage. In the 1960s, with the civil rights movement and the anti-war movement in full swing, young people who were rebelling against authority loved folk songs. Presley, who appeared to be **submissive** to the establishment, was no longer their hero.

Presley resumed full-scale live concerts in 1969 after an eight-year absence.   25
He began a hectic and stressful period, which caused many difficulties. His wife grew lonely in his absence and left him, taking their young daughter. Presley himself suffered from great personal stress and loneliness. To treat his mental and physical **ailments**, he took a variety of medications, which became increasingly dangerous. He also had another serious problem: bulimia.   30

Presley had always struggled to control his weight. He loved to eat, and eating relieved his anxiety and his sense of isolation. One of his favorite foods was peanut butter, banana and bacon on a sandwich. Now, it's often referred to as an Elvis sandwich in restaurants around America. It was his mother's habit to make this for him, and it was comfort-food from his childhood. Perhaps he wanted to   35
eat it, even though he knew it was too high in calories to eat every day.

On 16 August 1977, Presley was found lying unconscious, on the floor of his bathroom at home. He was immediately rushed to hospital, but it was too late. The King had passed away. Although he had achieved the American dream, **amassing** a vast fortune and great fame, his isolation was not alleviated. How-   40
ever, his songs have certainly helped countless people to heal their loneliness.

📖 Notes ─────────────────────────────────

l. 1 **the embodiment:** 体現者

l. 2 **Bob Dylan:** ボブ・ディラン (1941-)、アメリカの歌手 (12章を参照のこと)

l. 2 **Freddie Mercury:** フレディ・マーキュリー (1946-1991)、イギリスのロックバンド・クイーンのボーカリスト、『ボヘミアン・ラプソディー』などのヒット曲がある

l. 7 **Tupelo:** テューペロ (ミシシッピ州の北東部にある都市)

l. 9 **Memphis:** メンフィス (テネシー州の南西端にある都市)

l. 20 **enlisted in the army:** 当時のアメリカは徴兵制が敷かれていた

l. 21 **the civil rights movement:** 公民権運動

l. 22 **in full swing:** 最高潮で

☑ Vocabulary Check

Match the following words from the reading passage with their correct definition.

1. achieve ( ) **a.** show that you don't like something
2. tinge ( ) **b.** gradually gather a large amount over time
3. enthusiastic ( ) **c.** succeed with effort, skill or courage
4. disapprove ( ) **d.** willing to obey without arguing
5. submissive ( ) **e.** a slight illness
6. ailment ( ) **f.** showing strong excitement
7. amass ( ) **g.** give a small amount of color or emotion to something

🔍 Reading Comprehension

Circle T if the sentence is true or F if it is false.

[T / F] **1.** Presley made his debut as a singer just after graduating from high school.

[T / F] **2.** As he lost his popularity, Presley enlisted in the army.

[T / F] **3.** In the 1960s, many young people were submissive to authority.

[T / F] **4.** Presley loved to eat, because eating relieved his anxiety and loneliness.

[T / F] **5.** Though Presley himself suffered from isolation, his songs helped many people to heal their loneliness..

🎧 Listening Comprehension

Listen and choose the correct answer.

17

1. Why was it fortunate for Presley to move from Tupelo to Memphis?

(A)   (B)   (C)

2. What caused conservative people to have a strong dislike for Presley?

(A)   (B)   (C)

3. Why was Presley suddenly no longer a hero of young people?

(A)   (B)   (C)

✍ Idioms and Expressions

Choose the correct phrase to complete each sentence.

1. The life of the wandering minstrel is (   ) loneliness and sadness.

2. In recent years people have been (   ) an increasingly large amount of information online.

3. They made their costumes (   ), and staged the musical for children.

4. Her parents (   ) her studying music abroad.

5. As Noah has a huge vocabulary, he is often (   ) as a walking dictionary.

> disapproved of   referred to   exposed to   at their own expense
> tinged with

💬 Enjoy the Dialogue!

Listen and fill in the blanks in the conversation below.

🎧 18

Lily: What are you doing for the Christmas holidays?

James: We're having a big family 1 _____ in Tennessee. It's the first time for me, and we're visiting Graceland.

Lily: Graceland? Elvis Presley's huge 2 _____ ? I didn't know you were a fan!

James: Me? Nah. But my grandpa is. We are doing a tour, then getting together with some 3 _____ later for Christmas dinner, Elvis style.

Lily: Ha ha! Sounds 4 _____ . I wish I could come.

James: You know, I don't think my family would 5 _____ me bringing my best friend at all. Let me message my grandparents and ask.

Lily: That would be 6 _____ . I have always wanted to see Graceland and I would love to meet your family.

James: Grandma messaged me right back! Get 7 _____ for gravy and mashed potatoes with everything, and my grandpa singing *Heartbreak Hotel* while he drives us around, woo!

Chapter 10

Aretha Franklin & Soul Food

「クイーン・オブ・ソウル」と称されたアレサ・フランクリン（1942-2018）は、ソウル、ゴスペル、R&Bなど幅広いジャンルで活躍したアメリカの歌手である。

📖 Reading Passage

For an American vocalist, it is a great honor to perform at a presidential inauguration. Aretha Franklin, dubbed the 'Queen of Soul', sang for President Carter in 1977, for President Clinton in 1997 and for President Obama in 2009. This shows how long she has been loved and recognized as a **formidable** singer.

Franklin was born in Memphis, Tennessee, in 1942. Her father was a very 5 well-known Baptist pastor and her mother was an accomplished gospel singer. As a child, she often sang gospel songs with her family in church. When she was six years old, her mother left the family and died suddenly of a heart attack four years later. She mourned her mother's death terribly. Gospel singing helped to **distract** her from her grief and loneliness. 10

Franklin was signed to Columbia Records at the age of 18 and moved to Atlantic Records six years later. The following year, she released *Respect*, which reached number one on the US charts. She quickly rose to star status and her heyday lasted into the mid-1970s, and in 1987 she became the first female artist to be **inducted** into the 'Rock and Roll Hall of Fame'. She won 20 Grammy 15 Awards and was presented with the Presidential Medal of Freedom in 2005.

Franklin's biggest hit, *Respect*, became an anthem for the civil rights and women's rights. Her father was an avid activist in the civil rights movement. He was one of its most influential leaders, along with Martin Luther King, Jr. Franklin was also a strong supporter of these social changes. Whenever called 20 upon, she willingly sang at political rallies. She stood by **vulnerable** people, and helped those in need of a voice.

Franklin liked to throw parties and treat her guests to soul food. This food has its roots in African-American cooking in the South, and was widely recognized as an ethnic traditional Southern cuisine in the1960s. Although it is 25 sometimes considered less healthy because of its high fat **content**, for African-Americans it is a style of cooking that creates deep **bonds**, of love and trust with family and friends.

Soul food consists of a wide variety of dishes: pork, fried chicken, chicken fried steak, fried fish, mashed potatoes, collard greens and lots of vegetables. 30 When Franklin met Pavarotti at a charity function, they hit it off and she invited him to a soul food party. Sadly, he had a prior engagement and could not accept her offer, but had he attended, he would have thoroughly enjoyed her hospitality.

Franklin was loved not only by fans, but also by famous musicians. The Beatles apparently wanted her to perform *Let It Be* at first. She **collaborated** 35 with many singers, including Elton John and Whitney Houston. In 2013, she was voted No. 1 on *Rolling Stone's* list of 100 greatest singers of all time, and 5 years later, she died of cancer at the age of 76. She and her songs will continue to be celebrated with great respect!

📖 Notes

l. 1 **a presidential inaguration:** 大統領就任式
l. 15 **Rock and Roll Hall of Fame:** ロックの殿堂、オハイオ州クリーブランドにある博物館
l. 15 **Grammy Awards:** グラミー賞
l. 16 **Presidential Medal of Freedom:** 大統領自由勲章（議会名誉黄金勲章と並ぶ最高位の勲章）
l. 19 **Martin Luther King, Jr.:** マーティン・ルーサー・キング・ジュニア（1929-1968）、バプテスト派の牧師（人種差別撤廃を訴え、公民権運動を指導）
l. 29 **chicken fried steak:** チキンフライドステーキ、牛肉に小麦粉の衣をまぶして揚げた料理（フライドチキンの作り方と似ているため、このような名前になった）
l. 31 **hit it off:** 会ってすぐに意気投合する
l. 33 **had he attended=if he had attended**
l. 37 ***Rolling Stone***:『ローリング・ストーン』（米国のカルチャー誌、音楽・政治・大衆文化などの記事を掲載する）

☑ Vocabulary Check

Match the following words from the reading passage with their correct definition.

1. formidable   (   )   **a.** strong feelings of friendship, love that unites people

2. distract   (   )   **b.** officially accept someone into an organization

3. induct   (   )   **c.** work together with someone

4. vulnerable   (   )   **d.** ingredients, or things inside something

5. content   (   )   **e.** take attention away from someone or something

6. bond   (   )   **f.** very powerful or impressive

7. collaborate   (   )   **g.** easily hurt physically or mentally

🔍 Reading Comprehension

Circle T if the sentence is true or F if it is false.

[T / F]   **1.** Gospel singing helped Franklin to overcome her grief and loneliness when her mother died.

[T / F]   **2.** Franklin's heyday lasted until she died at the age of 76.

[T / F]   **3.** Franklin's biggest hit, *Respect*, supported and encouraged vulnerable people.

[T / F]   **4.** Soul food has its roots in African-American cooking in the South.

[T / F]   **5.** Pavarotti attended a soul food party held by Franklin, and enjoyed her hospitality.

🎧 Listening Comprehension

Listen and choose the correct answer.

26

1. For whom did Franklin perform at a presidential inauguration for the first time?

    (A)   (B)   (C)

2. Why is soul food sometimes considered less healthy?

    (A)   (B)   (C)

3. When Franklin met Pavarotti at a charity function, where did she invite him?

    (A)   (B)   (C)

✍ Idioms and Expressions

Choose the correct phrase to complete each sentence.

1. Dr. Brown is (　　　　　　) one of the leading authorities on spacecraft design.
2. He volunteered (　　　　　　) his friends at the disaster site, to help clean up.
3. The voting system is (　　　　　　) a drastic reform.
4. The committee (　　　　　　) nine specialists on ecology and marine biology.
5. She (　　　　　　) overseas researchers to develop this new drug.

> consisted of　recognized as　along with　collaborated with　in need of

💬 Enjoy the Dialogue!

Listen and fill in the blanks in the conversation below.

🎧 **27**

Timothy: What have you got for lunch?

Naomi: I don't know, my mum packs my lunchbox really early every morning.

Timothy: Let's see then!

Naomi: Um, well, she has packed me a 1 ＿＿＿＿＿＿＿＿＿ bento. The 2 ＿＿＿＿＿＿＿＿＿ is rice and the top is pieces of carrot, fried chicken, a boiled egg, 3 ＿＿＿＿＿＿＿＿＿ and a taco wiener.

Timothy: Mmm . . . looks delicious! What's a taco wiener?

Naomi: This. It's a little sausage, cut into the shape of an 4 ＿＿＿＿＿＿＿＿＿ .

Timothy: Cute. It makes my peanut butter sandwich look a bit 5 ＿＿＿＿＿＿＿＿＿ .

Naomi: Yes, but my mum would never let me have sandwiches. I love peanut butter. She always goes the full traditional bento. I'll 6 ＿＿＿＿＿＿＿＿＿ with you, if you want.

Timothy: Really!? That would be great. Well, I don't think half a peanut butter sandwich is really 7 ＿＿＿＿＿＿＿＿＿ to a nice homemade bento.

<table>
<tr><td colspan="2">ミニ情報：アレサ・フランクリンと交流のあった歌手</td></tr>
<tr><td>Pavarotti: ルチアーノ・パヴァロッティ（1935-2007）、イタリアのオペラ歌手</td></tr>
<tr><td>Elton John: エルトン・ジョン（1947- ）、イギリスのシンガーソングライター</td></tr>
<tr><td>Whitney Houston: ホイットニー・ヒューストン（1963-2012）、アメリカの歌手・女優</td></tr>
</table>

Chapter 11   Seiji Ozawa & Nostalgic Nibbles

「世界のオザワ」と呼ばれる小澤征爾（1935- ）は、長年にわたって数々の海外の名門オーケストラを指揮し、世界中で高い評価を得ている日本人指揮者である。

📖 Reading Passage

28   Seiji Ozawa is a maestro, who has conducted **prestigious** orchestras internationally and in Japan. From his beginnings as a musician, he has been more highly regarded abroad, than in his home country. However, he has made a profound contribution to the popularity of classical music in Japan.

29   Ozawa was born in Shenyang, China, in 1935. He returned to Japan with 5 his mother and **siblings** at the age of 6. His father was a dentist, but his family loved music and encouraged him to become a pianist. He practiced the piano enthusiastically until one day, during a rugby match, he broke both of his index fingers. The injury was fatal to him as a pianist and his piano teacher advised him to become a conductor. 10

30   When Ozawa was a student at Toho Gakuen Junior College, he heard an American orchestra in concert. He was so struck by the conductor's command of the music that he wanted to go abroad to study. After graduation, opportunities to study overseas did not come easily. When he was at his wits' end, his friends came to his rescue and he was able to raise the **funds** to go to Europe, finally setting 15 off from the port of Kobe on a cargo ship to Marseilles, France, in 1959. Arriving

about 2 months later, he traveled to Paris on a scooter he had brought with him from Japan.

As soon as Ozawa arrived in Paris, a classmate from junior college informed him there was an international competition for young conductors in 4 months. He barely made it in time to apply but amazingly, he won the competition. The following year, he was given a prestigious prize for **promising** young conductors in the USA. With these successes, he was blessed to be taught by Karajan and Bernstein.

Few Japanese lived in Europe in the 1960s. Ozawa often visited these families and was treated to dinner. He was much obliged to his friends for their kindness, as he had **cravings** for Japanese cooking, especially when he was tired from work. Overseas, he missed Japanese food and asked his family to send him typical Japanese snacks and condiments: seaweed, pickled plums, sea urchins, soy sauce, wasabi powder and rice crackers.

Ozawa has served as musical director for several famous orchestras, 4 years with the Toronto Symphony Orchestra, 29 years with the Boston Symphony Orchestra and 8 years with the Vienna State Opera. Since founding his own music academy in 2000, he has been keen to **nurture** budding musicians, perhaps because he is very grateful for the support he received from people, when he was young.

In an interview, Ozawa was asked the message he would leave behind, for people 100 years from now. He said he hoped that war would **cease** to exist, and people around the world would understand each other. Cheerful, with a happy disposition he is much admired. His passion for music and his joy in performing make his conducting rich and inspiring!

📖 **Notes** ━━━━━━━━━━━━━━━━━━━━━━━━

l. 1 **maestro:** 名指揮者

l. 5 **Shenyang:** 瀋陽（中華人民共和国の東北地区の中心都市、旧称は奉天）

l. 11 **Toho Gakuen Junior College:** 桐朋学園短期大学（現在の桐朋学園大学）

l. 14 **at his wits' end:** 途方に暮れて

l. 16 **Marseilles:** マルセイユ（フランス南東部の港湾都市）

l. 32 **Toronto Symphony Orchestra:** トロント交響楽団（1922年設立、本拠地カナダ・トロント）

l. 32 **Boston Symphony Orchestra:** ボストン交響楽団（1881年創設、本拠地アメリカ・ボストン）

l. 33 **Vienna State Opera:** ウィーン国立歌劇場（1869年開場の世界で最も著名なオペラハウスの一つ）

l. 33 **his own music academy:** 小澤征爾音楽塾

☑ Vocabulary Check

Match the following words from the reading passage with their correct definition.

1. prestigious ( )
2. sibling ( )
3. fund ( )
4. promising ( )
5. craving ( )
6. nurture ( )
7. cease ( )

a. an amount of money that is collected for a special purpose

b. stop doing something

c. likely to be successful or good in the future

d. encourage people and help them to develop

e. inspiring, respected and admired, having high status

f. brother or sister

g. a very strong desire for something

⌕ Reading Comprehension

Circle T if the sentence is true or F if it is false.

[T / F] **1.** From his beginnings as a musician, Ozawa has been highly regarded both overseas and in Japan.

[T / F] **2.** Ozawa's family disapproved of his becoming a pianist.

[T / F] **3.** Ozawa went by ship on his first trip to Europe.

[T / F] **4.** Ozawa was fortunate to take lessons from internationally famous musicians.

[T / F] **5.** Ozawa has been the conductor for several prestigious orchestras for many years.

🎧 Listening Comprehension

Listen and choose the correct answer.

35

1. What caused Ozawa to want to go abroad to study?

   (A)   (B)   (C)

2. After arriving in Marseilles, how did Ozawa travel to Paris?

   (A)   (B)   (C)

3. When did Ozawa especially crave for Japanese food in Europe?

   (A)   (B)   (C)

44 At the Musician's Table: Food and Music

✍ Idioms and Expressions

Choose the correct phrase to complete each sentence.

1. She was (   ) the sheer beauty of the music at the concert last night.

2. He was just (   ) arrive for the concert, before the curtain rose.

3. I'm much (   ) him for his advice. I was at a loss for what to do.

4. My niece is (   ) join a professional soccer team.

5. Quite a few problems were (   ) when they returned to Japan suddenly.

> left behind   struck by   in time to   obliged to   keen to

💬 Enjoy the Dialogue!

Listen and fill in the blanks in the conversation below.

🎧 **36**

Harry: I think I'm all packed. Tent, tarp, sleeping bag, gas stove, fishing gear, and ₁ _____ pants.

Marc: How about food, in case we don't catch anything?

Harry: Oh! I never thought of that. I only have water and matches.

Marc: It's OK. I have a weeks' ₂ _____ of ready-to-eat meals in the back of the car for ₃ _____ .

Harry: Thanks. I feel a bit stupid, forgetting food. Sorry!

Marc: Well, I hope the fish are ₄ _____ , but if they're not, we have ravioli, lasagna and ₅ _____ beef with vegetables.

Harry: Thanks, you are definitely the more experienced fisherman today. Have you ever been to the camping site we're ₆ _____ for?

Marc: Yeah, quite a few times. It's about one hour and a half from here. The river and woods are really beautiful this time of year. It's usually good fishing. Fingers ₇ _____ !

ミニ情報：小澤征爾が師事した指揮者
Karajan: ヘルベルト・フォン・カラヤン（1908-1989）、オーストリアの指揮者（20世紀を代表する指揮者として、世界中で絶大な人気を誇った） **Bernstein**: バーンスタイン（2章の Notes を参照のこと）

Chapter 12   Bob Dylan & Country Pie

『風に吹かれて』などのヒット曲で知られるボブ・ディラン（1941-）は、音楽家として初めてノーベル文学賞を受賞した、アメリカを代表するミュージシャンである。

📖 Reading Passage

37
Each year, the announcement of the Nobel Prize winners captures the world's attention. News of the 2016 Nobel Prize in Literature winner was a big surprise to many, but the winner himself seemed more **astonished** than anyone. After two weeks' silence, Bob Dylan announced that he would accept the honor, but he did not attend the award ceremony. Incidentally, Kazuo Ishiguro, the 2017 ₅ Nobel Prize in Literature winner is a big fan of his music and poetry.

38
Dylan was born in 1941 in the northern Minnesota port town of Duluth. His paternal grandparents were Jewish **immigrants** from Odessa on the Black Sea coast. His maternal grandparents were also Jewish immigrants from Lithuania. He grew up in a happy house, with a good, supportive family environment. From ₁₀ an early age, he had a strong interest in music and dreamed of becoming a musician. He **adored** the music of Elvis Presley, and formed a rock and roll band with his friends.

39
Following his parents' advice, Dylan **enrolled** the University of Minnesota in 1959, but never could give up his dream of becoming a musician. The follow- ₁₅ ing winter, he left Minneapolis and arrived in New York in a heavy snowstorm.

Singing at coffeehouses and other **venues** in Greenwich Village, he got his debut opportunity. He signed with Columbia Records in 1961, and released his first album in 1962, which did not sell as well as expected.

In 1963, Dylan released the second album. It was a breakthrough for him. His biggest hit, *Blowin' in the Wind* was included on this album, and he established a widespread reputation as a singer-songwriter. There were very few singer-songwriters at the time. Thereafter, he received numerous awards including 11 Grammy Awards, and Pulitzer Prize Special Citations Awards. In 2012, President Barack Obama presented him with the Presidential Medal of Freedom at the White House.

In fact, it is not very surprising that Dylan won the Nobel Prize. There had been rumors since way back in 1996, that he was in the running for the award. He is very interested in literature and his songs are strongly influenced by poets and writers. He was a close friend of Allen Ginsberg, one of America's founding Beat poets. Ginsberg **praised** the lyrics of his songs, long before the Nobel Committee recognized that Dylan had created new poetic expressions within the great American song traditions.

Dylan rarely ever talks about himself. His personal life is **shrouded** in mystery. It's even difficult to find clues to his food preference. With the exception of *Country Pie*, he rarely mentions food in his songs. In the lyrics, are the names of fruits and vegetables used in pie making, such as blueberries, apples, cherries and pumpkins. It's probably the only hint we will ever get, that pie is his favorite food! Which one does he like best? The answer, my friend, is baking in the pie! The answer is baking in the pie!

📖 Notes ━━━━━━━━━━

l. 7 **Duluth:** ダルース（ミネソタ州北部の港町）

l. 8 **Odessa:** オデーサ（ウクライナ南部の黒海に面した港湾都市）

l. 8 **Black Sea:** 黒海（ヨーロッパとアジアの間にある内海）

l. 9 **Lithuania:** リトアニア共和国（バルト三国の一つ）

*l.*16 **Minneapolis:** ミネアポリス（ミネソタ州最大の都市）

*l.*17 **Greenwich Village:** グリニッチ・ヴィレッジ（ニューヨーク市マンハッタン区の一地区、当時は多くの芸術家が集まることで知られていた）

*l.*24 **Pulitzer Prize Special Citations Awards:** ピュリッツァー賞特別賞（ピュリッツァー賞とは報道・文学・音楽の分野における優れた業績に対して贈られる賞）

*l.*25 **Presidential Medal of Freedom:** 大統領自由勲章（10章の Notes を参照のこと）

*l.*28 **in the running for …:** ～の候補に挙がっている

☑ Vocabulary Check

Match the following words from the reading passage with their correct definition.

1. astonished ( )   **a.** love someone or something very much
2. immigrant ( )   **b.** officially become a member of an institution or course
3. adore ( )   **c.** say or write good things about someone or something
4. enroll ( )   **d.** the place where an event happens
5. venue ( )   **e.** a person who comes to live in a different country
6. praise ( )   **f.** hide or cover something
7. shroud ( )   **g.** feeling or showing great surprise or wonder

🔍 Reading Comprehension

Circle T if the sentence is true or F if it is false.

[T / F] **1.** All of Dylan's grandparents were immigrants from Europe.

[T / F] **2.** As a boy, Dylan was not interested in music, and dreamed of becoming a baseball player.

[T / F] **3.** Dylan released his first album in 1962, and it was a big hit.

[T / F] **4.** People recognize that Dylan produced new types of poetic expressions in his songs.

[T / F] **5.** Dylan often refers to his favorite food in his songs.

🎧 Listening Comprehension

Listen and choose the correct answer.
43

1. After the Nobel Prize winners were announced, how long did Dylan stay silent?

(A)   (B)   (C)

2. While waiting for his debut opportunity, what did Dylan do?

(A)   (B)   (C)

3. Why is it not surprising that Dylan won the Nobel Prize?

(A)   (B)   (C)

✐ Idioms and Expressions

Choose the correct word to complete each sentence.

1. The building of a highway has destroyed the natural (   ) in this area.

2. She was lucky enough to have the (   ) to go abroad for study.

3. Our company has made a major (   ) in solar power technology.

4. The sweet shop along the high street has a good (   ).

5. This rule applies to every member of this club without (   ).

> exception   reputation   opportunity   environment   breakthrough

💬 Enjoy the Dialogue!

Listen and fill in the blanks in the conversation below.

🎧 44

Lecturer: Today we'll be talking about SDGs, sustainable 1 _____ goals. Who can tell me what kinds of areas these are?

Kaito: Good morning, I'm Kaito, representing Japan. SDGs target ending 2 _____ and discrimination.

Lecturer: That's right, who else can tell us more about this 3 _____ ?

Thorsten: Hello, I'm Thorsten, representing Germany. The goal is to ensure that people have a safe and healthy 4 _____ .

Lecturer: That's also an excellent answer. How about some of you tell us what your country is doing to 5 _____ these ideas?

Sean: Hey everyone, I'm Sean for Australia. Ours supports sustainability, and 6 _____ the impacts of climate change.

Lecturer: That's an important point. How about some other countries?

Ruchika: Hello, I'm Ruchika, from India. We are working on food 7 _____ . Making sure India grows enough food for each person.

ミニ情報：ボブ・ディランを高く評価した文学者
Kazuo Ishiguro：カズオ・イシグロ（1954- ）イギリスの作家、長崎で生まれ5歳のときに渡英、1989年に『日の名残り』でブッカー賞を、2017年にノーベル賞文学賞を受賞 **Allen Ginsberg**: アレン・ギンズバーグ（1926-1997）、ビート・ジェネレーションを代表するアメリカの詩人

Chapter 13　Taylor Swift & her Shake Shake Shake

楽曲だけでなくライフスタイルでも大きな注目を集めるテイラー・スウィフト
（1989- ）は、社会的貢献にも積極的なアメリカのシンガーソングライターである。

📖 Reading Passage

45　　　Since her debut at the age of 16, Taylor Swift, one of the biggest stars in American pop music, has been a **dominant** force not only with her singing, but also in fashion and lifestyle. She is a strong favorite among young girls and also their mothers, which is a rare combination of popularity, across age groups. This is because she has always tried to be a good role model for the younger genera- 5 tion.

46　　　Swift was born in 1989 in the small town of Wyomissing, Pennsylvania. Her father was a stockbroker and her mother, a businesswoman. She inherited her musical talent from her grandmother, who was a professional opera singer. Her parents were supportive of her efforts to fulfill her dream of becoming a vocalist. 10 Her mother supported her when she was **bullied** at school. She grew up in a happy, loving family environment.

47　　　Swift made her debut as a country musician and pioneered the country-pop genre, winning countless honors, including 11 Grammy Awards. She writes lyrics and bases her songs on her own experiences. Young girls can therefore relate to 15 and be inspired by her songs. Swift is renowned for her relationship with her fans, known as the 'Swifties' or 'Taylor Nation'. She effectively uses social media including blogs, Instagram and Twitter to **interact** with her fans. She sometimes invites a select few fans to parties and treats them to homemade cookies.

48

Although Swift is one of the most influential and wealthy celebrities, her food 20 preferences seem to **resemble** those of an average American young person. She likes ice cream, cookies and muffins. She is interested in organically grown food, but is never too strict with herself about what she eats and drinks. She loves Diet Coke and Starbucks drinks. In one interview, she said she orders a cheeseburger, fries and a chocolate shake at the drive-thru when she is out to eat. 25

49

Swift has started selling collaborative products. It is very typical of her to offer dresses and merchandise at **affordable** prices so that young people can purchase them. She really seems to understand her fan base and her market well. She has achieved great success, not only as a performer but also as a business-woman. She is now the **subject** of academic research. An institute at New York 30 University has set up a course for students to take lectures on her; in 2022, New York University awarded her an honorary doctorate in fine arts.

For a long time, Swift has remained silent on politics, but in 2018 she an-nounced that she would vote for the Democratic candidate. For a young country musician in a conservative neighborhood, **publicizing** her political beliefs can 35 be very risky. Many conservative voters boycott artists who don't hold the same political views. She has also spoken out against sexism and violations of LGBTQ rights and encouraged many people who need help. She has even taken direct action to help young musicians in financial need. Taylor Swift continues as a fine role-model for everyone. 40

📖 Notes ━━━━━━━━━━━━━━━━━━

l. 5 **role model:** お手本

l. 7 **Wyomissing, Pennsylvania:** ペンシルベニア州ワイオミッシング

l. 21 **those = the food preferences**

l. 24 **Starbucks:** スターバックス（1971年にシアトルで開業した世界最大のコーヒーチェーン店）

l. 30 **New York University:** ニューヨーク大学（1831年に設立されたニューヨーク市マンハッタン区にある私立大学）

l. 34 **Democratic:** 民主党の

l. 37 **sexism:** 性差別

l. 37 **LGBTQ:** Lesbian, Gay, Bisexual, Transgender, Questioning の頭文字を取って作られた言葉、性的マイノリティの総称の一つ

☑ Vocabulary Check

Match the following words from the reading passage with their correct definition.

1. dominant ( )   **a.** make something widely known to the public
2. bully ( )   **b.** the person or thing that is studied or discussed
3. interact ( )   **c.** more powerful, successful or influential
4. resemble ( )   **d.** hurt or threaten those they perceive as vulnerable
5. affordable ( )   **e.** talk or do things with other people
6. subject ( )   **f.** cheap enough for ordinary people to buy
7. publicize ( )   **g.** look like or be similar to someone or something

🔍 Reading Comprehension

Circle T if the sentence is true or F if it is false.

[T / F]   **1.** Taylor Swift's parents encouraged her to fulfil her dream of becoming a musician.

[T / F]   **2.** Taylor Swift made her debut as a rock singer.

[T / F]   **3.** Taylor Swift hoped to offer luxurious and expensive dresses and merchandise as collaborative products.

[T / F]   **4.** New York University has highly evaluated Taylor Swift's achievements.

[T / F]   **5.** Taylor Swift is critical of discrimination and respectful of human rights.

🎧 Listening Comprehension

🎧 **Listen and choose the correct answer.**

51

1. Why is Taylor Swift popular among young girls and also their mothers?

   (A)   (B)   (C)

2. Why are young girls inspired by Taylor Swift's songs?

   (A)   (B)   (C)

3. What are Taylor Swift's food preferences like?

   (A)   (B)   (C)

✍ Idioms and Expressions

Choose the correct phrase to complete each sentence. Each phrase can be used only once.

1. She was very (   ) us when we started this new project.
2. We were greatly (   ) his advice while we worked on this plan.
3. This area is (   ) the beauty of its mountains and wild alpine plants.
4. It is (   ) this kind of rabbit to dig burrows to live in.
5. The committee was (   ) to discuss school festival planning.

> inspired by   typical of   renowned for   supportive of   set up

💬 Enjoy the Dialogue!

Listen and fill in the blanks in the conversation below.

🎧
52

Erica: Hi Heidi. Do you want to come and sit with us?

Heidi: Sure. I have to go get lunch first. Um, how do I order at the cafeteria? It's my first time.

Erica: Oh, I didn't know you had never had cafeteria food. Don't worry, I'll go with you.

Heidi: Thanks. I'm a little 1 _____ . I haven't used my lunch card at all this year. What's the food like here?

Erica: It's pretty good. We have a different lunch special every day. Today is Taco Tuesday, so mostly Mexican food, and a good 2 _____ of vegetarian stuff. You just take a tray, have your lunch card ready, and the ladies 3 _____ the counter will help you.

Heidi: OK. Hi, can I get a bean and cheese burrito? With 4 _____ cream, guacamole, and extra salsa, please. Thank you.

Erica: You should grab a drink and some dessert. Just take it out of the 5 _____ , and put it on your tray, grab some chips or snacks, and 6 _____ your card at the 7 _____ . Easy peasy lemon squeezy!

Heidi: Hahaha! Thanks, it was easy. I love Mexican food. I am so glad you came with me the first time.

Chapter 14 Billy Eilish & Veganism

次々と音楽賞の最少年受賞者記録を塗り替えているビリー・アイリッシュ (2001-) は、社会問題にも高い意識を持つアメリカのシンガーソングライターである。

📖 Reading Passage

53
    Billy Eilish has broken numerous music records since the release of her debut single *Ocean Eyes* in 2016. She became the youngest artist to sing a *James Bond* theme song in 2020. *No Time to Die*, which she wrote with her brother Finneas, reached number 1 in the UK Singles Chart. That same year, she also became the youngest person to win 4 major Grammy Awards, breaking Taylor Swift's record. ₅

54
    Eilish was born in 2001 in Los Angeles, California. Both her father and mother are actors. Her parents respected their children's independence and freedom to pursue their interests. Billie and her brother who is four years older, were home-schooled by their parents. She enjoyed dancing, gymnastics and horse-riding. Although she did not come from a very wealthy family, she had an active ₁₀ and loving childhood, and grew up in a very close family unit.

55
    Eilish owes much of her success to her family, as well as her **exceptional** musical talent. She co-produces songs with her brother, whom she calls her best friend. Her parents take on roles as staff when she tours. They all work together to support her, but do not **interfere** excessively. Her family understands, respects ₁₅ and loves each other.

A successful singer at a very young age, Eilish has caught people's attention not only for her music but also for her fashion. Some admired her bulky, oversized style, while others **criticized** it. Her philosophy is to wear what she wants to wear. She does not want to be molded or stereotyped. Hence, she has recently 20 been experimenting with different types of fashion. However, she never wears fur clothing. As an animal rights activist, she is calling for an end to the use of real fur, and is very vocal about the subject.

 Because of her parents and their vegetarian diet, Eilish used to be a vegetarian, but is now a vegan. She has never eaten meat and does not eat **dairy** prod- 25 ucts at all. She loves vegetables and fruit, especially avocados. She once wanted to work at Jamba Juice. Her favorite foods include bean burritos, vegan chicken and choc-chip cookies. On tour, she **provides** vegetarian meals for other artists and staff and uses tableware that can be reused or composted. She is very conscious of environmental protection. Just like her contemporary, the Swedish environ- 30 mental activist, Greta Thunberg.

 Frankness is part of her appeal. She has **disclosed** to her fans that she has Tourette's Syndrome and received therapy for depression. Her honesty has encouraged her followers as much as her songs. She is also very concerned about social issues. She has been calling on young people to vote in elections. She has 35 expressed strong dissatisfaction with the government's gun control and global warming **initiatives**.

 Eilish wants to make the world a better place. We will keep an eye on her courageous words and actions. At the same time, we will be looking forward to watching her set new records one after another in the music world. 40

📑 Notes

l. 2 ***James Bond***: 『ジェームズ・ボンド』、イギリスの秘密諜報部員ジェームズ・ボンドを主人公とするスパイ映画シリーズ

l. 27 **Jamba Juice**: ジャンバジュース（スムージーのチェーン店、カリフォルニア州に本社がある）

l. 31 **Greta Thunberg**: グレタ・トゥーンベリ（2003- ）、スウェーデンの環境活動家

l. 33 **Tourette's Syndrome**: トゥレット症候群（運動性チックや音声チックが出現する神経系の疾患）

☑ Vocabulary Check

Match the following words from the reading passage with their correct definition.

1. exceptional ( )   **a.** give information to the public that was previously hidden
2. interfere ( )   **b.** things made from milk
3. criticize ( )   **c.** handle or adjust something without permission
4. dairy ( )   **d.** express disapproval of someone or something
5. provide ( )   **e.** the power or opportunity to act or take charge before others do
6. disclose ( )   **f.** unusually excellent
7. initiative ( )   **g.** give someone something that they want or need

⊙ Reading Comprehension

Circle T if the sentence is true or F if it is false.

[T / F]   **1.** Billie Eilish went to a local public school.

[T / F]   **2.** No one ever criticizes her fashion because Billie Eilish wears what she wants to wear.

[T / F]   **3.** Billie Eilish thinks people should respect the rights of animals.

[T / F]   **4.** Billie Eilish is very conscious of environmental protection and uses tableware that can be reused or composted.

[T / F]   **5.** Billie Eilish has the same opinion about global warming as Greta Thunberg.

🎧 Listening Comprehension

Listen and choose the correct answer.

1. What kind of fashion does Billie Eilish like?

(A)   (B)   (C)

2. What kind of food does Billie Eilish like?

(A)   (B)   (C)

3. What has Billie Eilish expressed her dissatisfaction to the government about?

(A)   (B)   (C)

✍ Idioms and Expressions

Choose the correct phrase to complete each sentence.

1. Last month she (   ) the position in charge of the research group.
2. They (   ) different fuel mixtures for the new engine.
3. Lots of musicians (   ) donations, to help victims of the earthquake.
4. When I was young, I (   ) enjoy camping by the river in summer.
5. I (   ) the pot of spaghetti, to make sure it didn't boil over.

> called for   took on   kept an eye on   used to   experimented with

💬 Enjoy the Dialogue!

Listen and fill in the blanks in the conversation below.

🎧 **Ms. Forge:** Welcome to the Summer Camp for outdoor skills introductory talk. In the next 3 weeks, we will all be learning basic camping. Yes, Tom?
61

Tom: Ms. Forge, will we need to pack food and our own camping gear? Or will all the meals and 1 _____ be provided?

Ms. Forge: A good question Tom, thanks for asking. We have emergency rations for everyone, for at least two months, but the 2 _____ of the camp is to forage and find food to 3 _____ for yourself.

Tom: So, what about equipment?

Ms. Forge: Well, we will be providing all the camping, cooking, fishing and safety equipment, 4 _____ the Summer Camp.

Tom: Ms. Forge, will there be any climbing or kayaking 5 _____ ? I love to kayak, but I have never gone climbing.

Ms. Forge: We have a river and kayaking 6 _____ , and at the camp site, we have a 7 _____ climbing wall to use.

Tom: Thanks! I am so excited to get going tomorrow morning!

Chapter 1: Quiz

I 文末の（　　）内の動詞を正しい形に直して下線部に入れ、英文を完成させなさい。

1. More than 50 years have passed since the Beatles _____ up in 1970. (break)

2. Young people felt _____ out and abandoned by a deceptively affluent community. (leave)

3. John and the orphans must have felt some sadness and loneliness at not _____ able to live with their parents. (be)

4. The four members of the Beatles may also _____ _____ strawberries and cream. (enjoy)

5. The multimedia company _____ by the Beatles is not 'Strawberry', but surprisingly it is 'Apple'. (found)

II 下線部の語と反対の意味を持つ語を、下の選択肢（動詞は原形、名詞は単数形で表記）から選びなさい。

1. In a short time, they acquired a very large and <u>enthusiastic</u> fan base.

   _____

2. The <u>conservatives</u> of the 1960s raised their eyebrows at the Beatles' critical and sometimes contemptuous attitude to authority.

   _____

3. About 28 tons of strawberries are <u>consumed</u> each year, during the two weeks of the festival.

   _____

4. Their name was coined by <u>combining</u> the word 'beat' with the insect 'beetle'.

   _____

5. It's a <u>funny</u> name, just like John, Paul, George and Ringo, who loved music and humor.

   _____

produce	indifferent	serious
divide	progressive	

Chapter 2: Quiz

I 最も適切な前置詞を下の選択肢から選んで空欄に入れ、英文を完成させなさい。ただし、必要に応じて大文字に変えること。

1. Hemming was born in Berlin (　　　　　) a Swedish architect father and a Japanese pianist mother in 1932.
2. When she was eighteen, she went (　　　　　) a painful experience.
3. She was deprived (　　　　　) her Swedish nationality, because she had never lived there.
4. When she got to Berlin, it was (　　　　　) a refugee of the Red Cross.
5. She doesn't want perfectionism in her music, but joy, passion and expression (　　　　　) all else.
6. (　　　　　) the same token, her love for music, and her care for animals and those less fortunate have made her career much more captivating.

as	of	to	by	above	through

II 文末の（　　）内の語を正しい形に直して下線部に入れなさい。

1. She is currently enjoying _____ around the world. (popular)

2. She experienced discrimination and extreme _____ in Berlin. (poor)

3. When her solo concert was planned on Bernstein's _____ , she was struck down by another ordeal. (recommend)

4. She managed to make a _____ by giving piano lessons in Germany for many years. (live)

5. She overcame the _____ of despair and has gained fame and wealth. (deep)

Chapter 3: Quiz

I 文末の日本語の意味になるように下線部に適語を入れ、英文を完成させなさい。

1. _____ _____ _____ , he carried on touring and visited many European countries. (その時から)

2. His father wanted him to be a court musician, and he spent about _____ _____ _____ his life traveling. (〜の3分の1)

3. In Vienna, he was often invited to luxurious dinners by the nobility, _____ _____ _____ the wealthy and affluent. (〜はもちろん)

4. He told his father he would present it to an acquaintance, _____ _____ _____ reward her for her kindness. (〜するために)

5. When his father sent him salted beef tongue, Mozart used half as a gift, and happily shared _____ _____ _____ for dinner with his wife. (残りの半分)

II 文末の（　）内の語を正しい形に直して下線部に入れなさい。

1. At the age of five, Mozart began to compose, and his father believed in his son's prodigious musical _____ . (able)

2. At the age of just six, he gave a performance in the _____ of Maria Theresa and Marie Antoinette in Vienna. (present)

3. When he was twenty-five years old, he moved to Vienna where he lived for the next ten years, until his _____ . (die)

4. He enjoyed a countless _____ of lavish, fancy food in many European cities. (various)

5. He craved the things he ate in his _____ , and asked his father in Salzburg to send some beef tongue. (young)

Chapter 4: Quiz

I 最も適切な動詞を下の選択肢から選んで空欄に入れ、英文を完成させなさい。

1. He visited and performed in many European countries: France, Italy, Switzerland, Germany, and England to (　　　　　　) a few.

2. His father was a thrifty person and didn't like to (　　　　　　) a lot of money on food.

3. As he became more well-known, he was invited to (　　　　　　) in a much more luxurious manner.

4. In the eighteenth century, royalty and nobility had begun to (　　　　　　) fruits in greenhouses in Europe.

5. What captivated his heart and occupied his mind most was to (　　　　　　) undying fame as a musician.

cultivate	attain	spend	name	dine

II 文末の日本語の意味になるように下線部に適語を入れ、英文を完成させなさい。

1. Mozart and his father would often _____ _____ _____ simple and inexpensive meals. （～で間に合わせる）

2. Contamination and general unsanitary conditions meant that even children drank beer or wine, diluted with hot water and _____ _____ Mozart. （モーツァルトもそうだった）

3. As he grew older, he loved not only beer and wine, _____ _____ champagne and punch. （～だけでなく…も）

4. Naturally, fruits grown in greenhouses were _____ _____ reach for the common people. （手が届かない）

5. _____ _____ his wife, he was not particular about his food. （～に依ると）

Chapter 5: Quiz

I 指示に従って答えなさい。

1. 最も適切な語を下の選択肢から選んで下線部に入れなさい。
You will hear Symphony No. 9 _____ every Christmastime.
    (play / playing / played / to play)

2. 最も適切な語を文末の選択肢から選んで下線部に入れなさい。
Early in his young life, an organist at the court took Beethoven _____ his wing, and helped him to improve his musical ability. (by / on / under / with)

3. 文末の (　　) 内の語を正しい形に直して下線部に入れなさい。
The visit was cut short, and he _____ _____ _____ go back to Bonn. (oblige)

4. 文末の (　　) 内の語を正しい形に直して下線部に入れなさい。
He despaired in the agony of _____ his hearing. (lose)

5. 「恋したかもしれない」という意味になるように fall を正しい形にして入れなさい。
He gave piano lessons to aristocratic women, and _____ _____ _____ in love with a few of them.

II 下線部の語とほぼ同じ意味を持つ語（句）を、下の選択肢から選びなさい。

1. Much of his work <u>still</u> remains extremely popular, about 200 years after his death.

　　　　　　　　　　　　　　　　　　　_____

2. Of all the classical musicians, his works are the most <u>frequently</u> performed.

　　　　　　　　　　　　　　　　　　　_____

3. Six years later he visited Vienna again, and decided to settle there <u>permanently</u>.

　　　　　　　　　　　　　　　　　　　_____

4. He was <u>remarkably</u> particular about the freshness of eggs.

　　　　　　　　　　　　　　　　　　　_____

5. He <u>occasionally</u> cooked for his guests when he invited them to dinner.

　　　　　　　　　　　　　　　　　　　_____

often	for good	sometimes	even now	unusually

Chapter 6: Quiz

I 最も適切な語を下の選択肢から選んで空欄に入れ、英文を完成させなさい。

1. In the winter of 1901, Rentaro Taki caught a severe cold, and was _____ to hospital in Leipzig, Germany.

2. During his eight months in hospital, his health _____ further.

3. In the following year, with little improvement in his condition, he was _____ to return home to Japan.

4. *Kojo no Tsuki* and *Hakone-Hachiri* were _____ as songs for junior high school music classes.

5. As his friends, they were very _____ for his health and took good care of him.

forced	concerned	adopted	admitted	deteriorated

II 文中の下線部の語を、指示された品詞に直しなさい。

1. As only the third person to study music abroad in the Meiji period, this was a great <u>honor</u>. 　　　　　形容詞 _____

2. He had only been studying in Germany a year and three months, and his ill health cut short his <u>ambitions</u> in Europe. 　　　　　形容詞 _____

3. He had been sent as an official student to Europe, by the Japanese <u>government</u>. 　　　　　動詞 _____

4. His sudden death was a huge <u>loss</u> for music education in the Meiji period. 　　　　　動詞 _____

5. Did the pickles he <u>received</u> cheer him up? 　　　　　名詞 _____

6. His friends hoped he would <u>recover</u> and return to study with them again in Leipzig. 　　　　　名詞 _____

Chapter 7: Quiz

I 最も適切な語（句）を文末の選択肢から選んで下線部に入れなさい。

1. Have you ever heard of the International Chopin Piano Competition, _____ is held every five years in Warsaw, Poland? (when / where / which)

2. After _____ from the Warsaw Conservatory in 1829, Chopin traveled with his friends to Vienna. (graduate / graduated / graduating)

3. _____ on his dreams for success in Vienna, Chopin left for Paris in 1831. (Given up / Has Given up / Having given up)

4. Before long, he was invited to the salons of the wealthy and aristocratic, _____ he gave elegant piano performances. (where / who / how)

5. They gradually became _____ to each other, and eventually began to live together in 1838. (attracted / attracting / to attract)

6. Chopin, who _____ Poland at the age of 20, finally returned to his beloved native land, after 20 years away. (would leave / has left / had left)

II 文末の（　）内の語を正しい形に直して下線部に入れなさい。

1. His father wanted him to acquire a wide range of _____ and to become cultured. (know)

2. The uprising in Poland, happening shortly after Chopin's _____ from Warsaw, created bad feelings towards the Poles. (depart)

3. He became one of the most sought-after piano teachers in Paris, achieving financial _____ . (secure)

4. Due to her _____ , he survived ill health and was able to concentrate on his musical career. (devote)

5. The relationship between Chopin and Sand came to an end in 1847, when he fell into a state of intense _____ and deep loneliness. (anxious)

Chapter 8: Quiz

I 下線部の語に接頭辞をつけて反対の意味の語を作りなさい。（例：regular → irregular）

1. His father wanted him to have a <u>practical</u> profession, and also to enjoy music as much as he did. _____

2. Dvořák was a dutiful son, so he <u>obediently</u> trained to become a butcher and learned German. _____

3. They admired each other and their relationship, like that of a father and son, <u>continued</u> throughout their lives. _____

4. He traveled to foreign countries, and gave <u>successful</u> concerts. _____

5. One of the most <u>famous</u> Czech dishes, is roast pork, pickled cabbage and knedlíky. _____

II 最も適切な語を下の選択肢から選んで空欄に入れ、英文を完成させなさい。

1. Fortunately for him, his German teacher (   ) his father to send him to music school.

2. A couple of years later, he joined the orchestra (   ) to the National Theatre.

3. Shortly after this, Bedřich Smetana was (   ) conductor of the theater, and Dvořák was strongly influenced by his musical style.

4. He was fortunate enough to be (   ) a public scholarship in 1875.

5. He (   ) to spend time at home with his family, rather than attend parties.

6. Knedlíky are dumplings that are (   ), then steamed or boiled.

appointed	attached	preferred
kneaded	awarded	persuaded

Chapter 9: Quiz

I 最も適切な前置詞を下の選択肢から選んで空欄に入れ、英文を完成させなさい。

1. His success story often seems to be tinged (　　　　　) sorrow.
2. Conservative people disapproved (　　　　　) his flamboyant performances on stage.
3. Young people who were rebelling (　　　　　) authority loved folk songs.
4. Presley resumed full-scale live concerts in 1969 (　　　　　) an eight-year absence.
5. Presley himself suffered (　　　　　) great personal stress and loneliness.
6. It's often referred (　　　　　) as an Elvis sandwich in restaurants around America.

against	from	of	to	with	after

II 指示に従って答えなさい。

1. 最も適切な語を文末の選択肢から選んで下線部に入れなさい。
   At the age of 13, his family moved to Memphis, Tennessee, _____ was very fortunate for him. (who / which / where / that)

2. 「自費で」という意味になるように下線部に適語を入れなさい。
   One day he made a record at _____ _____ _____ for a small local record company.

3. 文末の（　　）内の語を正しい形に直して下線部に入れなさい。
   In 1958, at the _____ of his popularity, Presley enlisted in the army. (high)

4. 「もはや～ない」という意味になるように下線部に適語を入れなさい。
   Presley, who appeared to be submissive to the establishment, was _____ _____ their hero.

5. 「たとえ～でも」という意味になるように下線部に適語を入れなさい。
   Maybe he wanted to eat it a lot, _____ _____ he knew it was too high in calories to eat every day.

Chapter 10: Quiz

I 下線部の語と反対の意味を持つ語を、下の選択肢から選びなさい。

1. Gospel singing helped to distract her from her <u>grief</u> and loneliness.

   _____

2. The <u>following</u> year, she released *Respect*, which reached number one on the US charts.

   _____

3. It is sometimes considered <u>less</u> healthy because of its high fat content.

   _____

4. Soul food consists of a <u>wide</u> variety of dishes.　　_____

5. Sadly, he had a prior engagement and could not <u>accept</u> her offer.

   _____

> refuse　　more　　narrow　　joy　　previous

II 指示に従って答えなさい。

1. 最も適切な語を文末の選択肢から選んで下線部に入れなさい。

   This shows _____ long she has been loved and recognized as a formidable singer. (what / which / why / how)

2. 文末の（　　）内の語を正しい形に直して下線部に入れなさい。

   She _____ 20 Grammy Awards and was presented with the Presidential Medal of Freedom in 2005. (win)

3. 文末の（　　）内の語を正しい形に直して下線部に入れなさい。

   Whenever _____ upon, she willingly sang at political rallies. (call)

4. 最も適切な語を文末の選択肢から選んで下線部に入れなさい。

   It is a style of cooking _____ creates deep bonds, of love and trust with family and friends. (who / what / when / that)

5. 接続詞を使って、同じ意味になるように下線部を書き直しなさい。

   <u>Had he attended</u>, he would have thoroughly enjoyed her hospitality.

   = _____ _____ _____ _____ , he would have thoroughly enjoyed her hospitality.

Chapter 11: Quiz

I 最も適切な語を下の選択肢から選んで空欄に入れ、英文を完成させなさい。

1. From his beginnings as a musician, he has been more highly regarded abroad, (   ) in his home country.

2. He practiced the piano enthusiastically (   ) one day, during a rugby match, he broke both of his index fingers.

3. He was so struck by the conductor's command of the music (   ) he wanted to go abroad to study.

4. Arriving about 2 months (   ), he traveled to Paris on a scooter he had brought with him from Japan.

5. He (   ) made it in time to apply but amazingly, he won the competition.

later	than	barely	that	until

II 最も適切な語を下の選択肢から選んで空欄に入れ、英文を完成させなさい。

1. The injury was (   ) to him as a pianist and his piano teacher advised him to become a conductor.

2. The following year, he was given a prestigious prize for (   ) young conductors in the USA.

3. With these successes, he was (   ) to be taught by Karajan and Bernstein.

4. Overseas, he missed Japanese food and asked his family to send him (   ) Japanese snacks and condiments.

5. Since founding his own music academy in 2000, he has been (   ) to nurture budding musicians.

promising	keen	blessed	fatal	typical

Chapter 12: Quiz

I 下線部の語とほぼ同じ意味を持つ語を、下の選択肢（動詞は原形で表記）から選びなさい。

1. Each year, the announcement of the Nobel Prize winners <u>captures</u> the world's attention.

   _____

2. He grew up in a happy house, with a good, <u>supportive</u> family environment.

   _____

3. He <u>adored</u> the music of Elvis Presley, and formed a rock and roll band with his friends.

   _____

4. His biggest hit, *Blowin' in the Wind* was included on this album, and he established a widespread <u>reputation</u> as a singer-songwriter.

   _____

5. With the exception of *Country Pie*, he <u>rarely</u> mentions food in his songs.

   _____

worship	seldom	attract	fame	helpful

II 文末の日本語の意味になるように下線部に適語を入れ、英文を完成させなさい。

1. The winner himself seemed more astonished _____ _____ .（誰よりも）

2. His paternal grandparents were Jewish _____ _____ Odessa on the Black Sea coast.（〜からの移民）

3. His first album did not sell _____ _____ _____ expected.（期待したほどには）

4. There were very _____ singer-songwriters at the time.（ほとんどいなかった）

5. _____ _____ , it is not very surprising that Dylan won the Nobel Prize.（実は）

6. Ginsberg praised the lyrics of his songs, _____ _____ the Nobel Committee recognized that Dylan had created new poetic expressions.（ずっと前に）

Chapter 13: Quiz

I 最も適切な語（句）を文末の選択肢から選んで下線部に入れなさい。

1. Since her debut, Swift _____ a dominant force not only with her singing, but also in fashion and lifestyle. (is / was / has been / had been)

2. She is a strong favorite among young girls and also their mothers, _____ is a rare combination of popularity, across age groups. (who / what / which / that)

3. Although Swift is one of the most influential and wealthy celebrities, her food preferences seem to resemble _____ of an average American young person. (that / those / one / ones)

4. She is interested in organically _____ food. (grow / grew / grown / growing)

5. It is very typical of her to offer dresses and merchandise at affordable prices _____ young people can purchase them. (how / so that / why / which)

II 文中の下線部の動詞を名詞形に直しなさい。

1. This is because she has always <u>tried</u> to be a good role model for the younger generation.   _____

2. She <u>inherited</u> her musical talent from her grandmother.   _____

3. Young girls can therefore relate to and be <u>inspired</u> by her songs.

    _____

4. She effectively <u>uses</u> social media including blogs, Instagram and Twitter to interact with her fans.   _____

5. She sometimes <u>invites</u> a select few fans to parties and treats them to homemade cookies.   _____

6. She has <u>achieved</u> great success, not only as a performer but also as a businesswoman.   _____

Chapter 14: Quiz

I 文末の（　　）内の語を正しい形に直して下線部に入れなさい。

1. Billy Eilish _____ _____ numerous music records since the release of her debut single *Ocean Eyes* in 2016. (break)

2. Although she did not come from a very wealthy family, she had an active and loving childhood, and _____ up in a very close family unit. (grow)

3. Hence, she has recently been _____ with different types of fashion. (experiment)

4. Because of her parents and their vegetarian diet, Eilish used to be a vegetarian, but _____ now a vegan. (be)

5. She uses tableware that can _____ _____ or composted. (reuse)

6. We will be looking forward to _____ her set new records one after another in the music world. (watch)

II 最も適切な語を下の選択肢から選んで空欄に入れ、英文を完成させなさい。

1. Eilish owes much of her success to her family, as well as her (　　　　　) musical talent.

2. As an animal rights activist, she is calling for an end to the use of real fur, and is very (　　　　　) about the subject.

3. She has never eaten meat and does not eat (　　　　　) products at all. She loves vegetables and fruit, especially avocados.

4. She is also very concerned about (　　　　　) issues.

5. We will keep an eye on her (　　　　　) words and actions.

dairy	social	exceptional	courageous	vocal

音楽家たちが奏でる食文化

検印
省略

© 2024 年 1 月 31 日　初版発行

著　者　　　　　　　　　堀越ウェンディ
　　　　　　　　　　　　松井真帆
　　　　　　　　　　　　本山ふじ子

発行者　　　　　　　　　小川洋一郎

発行所　　　　　　　株式会社　朝日出版社
　　　　　〒 101-0065　東京都千代田区西神田 3-3-5
　　　　　　　　　　　電話　(03) 3239-0271/72
　　　　　　　　　　　FAX　(03) 3239-0479
　　　　　　　　　　e-mail　text-e@asahipress.com
　　　　　　　　　URL　https://www.asahipress.com
　　　　　　　　　　　振替口座　00140-2-46008
　　　　　　　　　組版：ファースト／製版：錦明印刷